W9-BUP-821

Each year the New York Public Library and Oxford University Press invite a prominent figure in the arts, letters, or sciences to give a series of lectures on a topic of his or her choice. The lectures become the basis of a book jointly published by the Library and the Press. Distinguished American historian C. Vann Woodward, Sterling Professor of History Emeritus at Yale University, is the first in this series. His lectures were delivered in February and March of 1990.

THE OLD WORLD'S NEW WORLD

BOOKS BY C. VANN WOODWARD

Tom Watson: Agrarian Rebel (1938)

The Battle of Leyte Gulf (1947)

Reunion and Reaction (1951)

Origins of the New South, 1877–1913 (1951), Bancroft Prize, 1952

The Strange Career of Jim Crow (1955)

The Burden of Southern History (1960)

American Counterpoint (1971)

Thinking Back (1986)

The Future of the Past (1988)

The Old World's New World (1991)

EDITED BY C. VANN WOODWARD

George Fitzhugh: Cannibals All! (1960)

Lewis Blair: A Southern Prophecy (1964)

The Comparative Approach to American History (1968)

Responses of the Presidents to Charges of Misconduct (1974)

Mary Chesnut's Civil War (1981), Pulitzer Prize, 1982

The Private Mary Chesnut, with collaboration (1984)

THE
OLD WORLD'S
NEW WORLD

C. VANN WOODWARD

THE NEW YORK PUBLIC LIBRARY
OXFORD UNIVERSITY PRESS
New York · Oxford

1991

Oxford University Press

Oxford   New York   Toronto
Delhi   Bombay   Calcutta   Madras   Karachi
Petaling Jaya   Singapore   Hong Kong   Tokyo
Nairobi   Dar es Salaam   Cape Town
Melbourne   Auckland
and associated companies in
Berlin   Ibadan

Copyright © 1991 by C. Vann Woodward

Published jointly by The New York Public Library and Oxford University Press, Inc.

Oxford is a registered trademark of Oxford University Press

All rights reserved. No part of this publication may be reproduced,
stored in a retrieval system, or transmitted, in any form or by any means,
electronic, mechanical, photocopying, recording, or otherwise,
without the prior permission of Oxford University Press.

LIBRARY OF CONGRESS CATALOGING-IN-PUBLICATION DATA
Woodward, C. Vann (Comer Vann), 1908–
The Old World's new world / C. Vann Woodward.
p. cm.   Includes bibliographical references and index.
ISBN 0–19–506451–8
1. United States—Foreign public opinion, European.
2. Public opinion—Europe.   I. Title.
D1065.U5W66   1991   973—dc20
90–22893

1 3 5 7 9 8 6 4 2
Printed in the United States of America
on acid-free paper

For

PETER GAY

Preface

Nothing quite comparable to the great body of European commentary on America exists—that is, commentary both derogatory and laudatory directed at one nation by many contemporary nations during the last two centuries. To be sure, the French have written critically of the English, the English of the French, French of Germans and vice versa, and so all nations of Europe have written from time to time of one another. But they have done so from a different set of assumptions, expectations, and attitudes. They had grown more or less resigned to one another and accustomed to write about each other as peers and equals, or at least as contemporaries and neighbors, sometimes friendly, sometimes hostile.

When they turned to America, however—after the word "America" came commonly to mean the first independent republic in the New World—significant changes took place in tone and attitude. Something in the way of a generational break existed here. The United States was, after all, the first of the second generation of nation states in the western family of nations. It was but natural that nations of the older generation, those of the Old World, should have assumed parental roles of responsibility, discipline, and admonition, and it was only to be expected that the deferential tone assumed between equals should have sharpened at times to an admonitory edge. Their words were sometimes those of age to youth, parent to offspring, master to apprentice, teacher to pupil. From the very start the youth metaphor was built into European thinking about America, and there it stuck for hundreds of years. The

passage of centuries and the fading of youth, along with
youth's attributes—innocence as well as irresponsibility, gen-
erosity with prodigality—have made little difference. Over
and over, America was called the Land of the Future, more
often than not with a shudder.

The outpouring of European commentary and books on
America is not to be explained adequately in terms of Old
World sense of duty and concern for New World offspring.
Quite as important, perhaps, as an inducement for Europeans
to sound off on America was an intense concern and curiosity
of the offspring about what the Old World thought of them.
Much of what Europeans wrote on the subject was written in
shrewd awareness of this American market. Frances Trollope,
who profited handsomely from the opportunity, observed that
"one of the most remarkable traits in the national character of
the Americans" is "their exquisite sensitiveness and soreness
respecting every thing said or written concerning them." More
than thin-skinned, Americans seemed to have "no skins at
all."[1] Half a century later Matthew Arnold described the trait
as "a *tic*, a mania, which everyone notices" in Americans.[2]

Again and again European visitors, particularly in the
nineteenth century, were confronted with some variation of
the embarrassing question, "What do you think of us upon the
whole?" To Captain Basil Hall it was put "every day, and
almost in every company," and more often than not it took the
form, "Don't you think this is a wonderful country?"[3] The
desired and expected response to such questions was of course
affirmative and laudatory. When the published response
turned out to be the opposite, as it often did, this did not
diminish, but rather whetted American interest. Hostile and
sensational books were likely to command more attention

---

[1] Frances Trollope, *Domestic Manners of the Americans*, ed. Donald Smalley
(New York, 1949; original ed., 1832), 354–58.
[2] Matthew Arnold, *Civilization in the United States. First and Last Impressions
of America* (Freeport, N.Y., 1972; reprint of original ed., 1888), 60–61.
[3] Captain Basil Hall, *Travels in North America in the Years 1827–1828* (2 vols.,
Philadelphia, 1829), I, 11, 239–40.

than sympthetic and serious books. Both kinds were in demand and both were produced in great quantities, along with all possible intermixtures.

It was natural that a large part of the American mind should have been made in Europe and that Americans should have looked to Europe for its precepts and mentors. That part of the American mind that houses self-esteem, confidence, and self-image has also been shaped and influenced by the stream of European analysis and criticism over the centuries. The influence continues to our own day.

To raise these questions is not to presume easy answers, nor to assume a defensive posture—certainly not to reject foreign criticism because it is foreign. That would be to commit the most egregious blunder of nationalism. It would also be to close our minds to some important insights into American life and history. For the subject has occasionally attracted intellects of high order, a few of them when fully engaged, along with the more numerous run of lightweights. Then there is something to the contention that for a long period virtually the only sources of unwelcome truth about American life were foreign.

Other societies, the few with freedom to do so, vented home truths of this type by criticism of their rulers and governors. That solution came harder to the self-governed, for criticism of the rulers then risks becoming self-criticism. Only absolute rulers have been accused of more intolerance of criticism than democratic majorities, or more proneness to self-flattery. That is a special reason for attention in a democracy to criticism from abroad. Speaking of majority rule in America, Alexis de Tocqueville wrote, "The majority lives in the perpetual utterance of self-applause, and there are certain truths which Americans can learn only from strangers or from experience."[4]

In his classic work, *Democracy in America*, Tocqueville

---

[4] Alexis de Tocqueville, *Democracy in America* (2 vols., New York, 1972; original Paris ed. Part I, 1835; Part II, 1840), I, 265.

began with the admission that he sought more than to satisfy a
curiosity or to benefit Americans by his criticism, and that he
hoped "to find there instruction by which we [Europeans] may
ourselves profit." He continued: "I confess that in America I
saw more than America; I sought there the image of democracy itself, with its inclinations, its character, its prejudices,
and its passions, in order to learn what we have to fear or to
hope from its progress." Before he was half finished with his
inquiry he was persuaded that "The question here discussed is
interesting not only to the United States, but to the whole
world; it concerns not a nation only, but all mankind."[5]

By 1835 Tocqueville had come reluctantly to believe that
the nations of Europe "will soon be left with no other alternative than democratic liberty or the tyranny of the Caesars."
Granting that "the wishes of democracy are capricious, its
instruments rude, its laws imperfect," granting as well an
appalling list of shortcomings that he abhorred—minds "so
petty, so insipid, so crowded with paltry interests"—Tocqueville still regarded democracy "not as the best, but as the only
means of preserving freedom."[6] It was not taste or preference
but necessity that drove him to this conviction, and it was a
necessity of his own world, not that of America, that he had
uppermost in mind. For his predecessors as for his successors
in the long roster of foreign critics of American democracy,
their subject often seemed to them pregnant in some degree
with the fate or the hope for wider horizons than those of the
western republic.

In the twentieth century, there are European nations that
have sought on the left or on the right an alternative other than
democracy, to what Tocqueville called "the tyranny of the
Caesars." And in the years since the Second World War, a
half-dozen East European countries adopted, or have been
coerced into adopting, the alternative that came from the east.

[5] Ibid., 14.
[6] Ibid., 326, 329.

Now that they have found little to choose between the "tyranny of the Caesars" and that of a modern kind and have overthrown or "reformed" their old governments out of existence, they have all—some with more success than others—turned back to the alternative to tyranny that Tocqueville reluctantly concluded was the only one available—democracy.

Of democracy there are many definitions and numerous models. Some of them we find hard to reconcile with our own definitions and conceptions. In choosing which model to follow, the newly proclaimed democracies of Europe will be especially attentive to that offered by America. Not only is it the most conspicuous example, but it is also the oldest surviving democracy in the world. All the European nations that are now in search of democratic models will have American relatives, descendants of immigrants they have been sending to the United States for centuries. The image of democracy these immigrants have formed in America and transmitted to the old countries will doubtless play a part in shaping contemporary images.

We can only hope that in weighing the worth of the American democracy as model for their own governments the newly self-liberated nations of East Europe will not fall prey to the propaganda that democratic salvation is guaranteed by the whims of the market, or that prosperity is a necessary consequence of democratic institutions. We also hope that the new European democracies will be cautious in permitting their views of America to be shaped by the opinions about the New World democracy that the Old World has been pouring forth for many years. One of the reasons for undertaking the study that follows is the hope that it may help to forestall mistaken impressions of the oldest democracy on the part of the youngest democracies in Western culture.

June 1991   C.V.W.

Contents

Introduction

For our sampling of European views of America we are dependent on those opinions that found written form and were preserved. Those not written or preserved, and therefore the opinions of the great majority, are beyond our reach. What remains is necessarily derived from the minority of those literate and articulate Europeans who took the pains to record and preserve their thoughts. While their works constitute a perfectly enormous library of writings of many varieties from all over Europe, they are predominantly the views of the upper or middle ranks of society, with meager representation of the lower ranks. It is well to remember also that these were Europeans of those centuries when Europe regarded itself as the center of all things, rightful superior of the rest of the world, and the very embodiment of "civilization" itself. They made no bones about looking down upon lesser breeds— including the pretensions of their own colonies and their former colonies in the New World.

Not all these writers deigned to visit America, but among those who did, and those who are more frequently quoted, are princes of the blood and nobles of high rank, scientists, artists, actors, historians, poets, novelists, and adventurers, revolutionists in exile, fugitives from justice, outcasts in disgrace, rulers deposed, dictators to be, prophets on the make, diplomats and labor leaders, salesmen and saints. Among them were a former king of Spain, a future king of France, the redoubtable Prince de Tallyrand, the son and two grandsons of Napoleon Bonaparte, and, among numerous revolutionists,

Garibaldi of Italy, Kossouth of Poland, and Bakunin and Trotsky of Russia.

France's part in the American Revolution, and America as precedent for France's Revolution, brought many French notables to our shores. The Marquis de Barbé-Marbois, secretary of the French Legation during the American Revolution and later a revolutionist in his own country, entitled his books on America *Our Revolutionary Forefathers*.[1] (Mind you, a ten-year-old nation of forefathers!) The Marquis de Lafayette played the transatlantic role of hero to both revolutions for half a century. The Marquis de Chastellux, friend of Voltaire and Gibbon, served America well, not only in a military capacity but, as savant and philosophe of the *Académie Française*, as one of its friendlier and shrewder observers.

The great flood of books on America by foreign residents, officials, visitors, and travelers did not begin until later, with those from Britain foremost. For example, in the twenty-five years before the American Civil War more than two hundred travel accounts appeared in Britain, and by that time more than fifty had been published in Germany, fifty-six in Norway, fourteen in Italy, eight in Hungary, and a substantial shelf from Poland and other countries. Books on America had become a major share of the European publishing industry by the middle of the nineteenth century. They often went through several printings in the first few months and were translated into several languages. Two French travel magazines, *Le Tour du Monde* and *Le Journal des Voyages*, flourished by featuring articles about America.[2]

Learned and unlearned, celebrated and obscure, high and low in social rank, on they came, notebook in hand, pen poised. A very mixed lot these Europeans were. From Britain

---

[1] François, Marquis de Barbé-Marbois, *Our Revolutionary Forefathers. The Letters During His Residence in the United States as Secretary of the French Legation, 1779–1785* (New York, 1929).

[2] Ray Allen Billington, *Land of Savagery/Land of Promise. The European Image of the American Frontier* (New York, 1981), 74.

few in the higher ranks of society felt impelled for a long time after losing two bruising wars with American upstarts, to visit the former colonies. But many British figures of distinction—and a prominence sometimes gained by what they wrote on America—did come. Novelists great and small, the Trollopes, mother and son, Charles Dickens, William Makepeace Thackeray, and later in the nineteenth and through the twentieth century men of letters in numbers followed them to America. Matthew Arnold, John Morley, and Rudyard Kipling stood out, and among those of science and learning were John Tyndall the physicist, Charles Lyell the geologist, Thomas Huxley the biologist, Herbert Spencer the sociologist, Edward Freeman the historian, and George Bernard Shaw the playwright. Comparable notables from the Continent who came and saw and wrote could be added to them, down to and including Sigmund Freud and Albert Einstein.

It is misleading, however, so far as our purpose is concerned, to give too much prominence to those who crossed the Atlantic and to neglect those who never did. Often it was those who never set foot on western shores, and were in no sense "travellers," who had the more memorable and famous things to say about "the strange New World"—sometimes, to be sure, simply because they were memorable and famous themselves. These included Montaigne, Shakespeare, Hobbes, Pope, Rousseau, Edmund Burke, Dr. Johnson, Goethe, Schiller, Blake, Wordsworth, Byron, Hegel, and Marx. None of these had a firsthand look at the New World, yet their words and thoughts might come more readily and frequently to mind than the words of those who came and saw. I repeat, it is not America, but European views about America that are under examination here. Whether they are illusion, fact, or fantasy, or whether acquired at home or abroad is not the important thing. Not what they reveal about Americans, but what they reveal about Europeans and their ideas of America are the main subject of our inquiry. Whatever contradictory or valid insights and perceptions they may have inspired concerning any period or aspect of American reality is quite incidental to our purpose, and there are usually better sources for such speculation.

It is not always as simple as it may seem to distinguish between Europeans and Americans. A famous essay was published in 1782 entitled "What Is an American?" by J. Hector St. John de Crèvecœur, as he renamed himself in America. It is a pity he did not write an essay on "What Is a European?" as well, for he admirably illustrates our problem by his own career. Crèvecœur spent the first twenty-four years in France, England, and Canada, the last twenty-four years of his life in Europe and only fifteen or so of the intervening years in America. Yet he entitled his book *Letters from an American Farmer.*[3] He had taken out citizenship papers in New York before it was published and evidently thought of himself as an American, using the pronouns "we," "us," and "ours" as if he were. But he was appointed French consul in 1789 at New York before he returned to France in 1790 to spend the rest of his life. A somewhat comparable instance is that of the present-day writer, J. Martin Evans, who has spent his first twenty-eight years in England, more time than that in America, and has published an absorbing book entitled *America: The View from Europe.*[4]

The painter John Butler Yeats, father of the poet William Butler Yeats, spent his last fifteen years trying to become an American, and wrote ruefully of his experiences. "A sort of European old-maidishness gets between me and them," he said. "Depend upon it, it is a mistake sometimes to have been too well brought up, it prevents you from realising that in America everything hitherto respected including your polite-

[3] J. Hector St. John de Crèvecœur, *Letters from an American Farmer* (Everyman's Ed., London, 1912; original ed., 1782). "What Is an American" appears here as Letter III.

[4] J. Martin Evans, *America: The View from Europe* (Stanford, 1976).

ness or reticence is quite out of date."[5] Professional anthropologists of Europe have not been of much help. Geoffrey Gorer, for example, tried to persuade us that the key to understanding the American experience is "the individual rejection of the European father as a model and a moral authority, which every second-generation American had to perform."[6]

What then is a European? We think of German-born Carl Schurz as American rather than European. Yet while German-born Francis Lieber, like Schurz settled in America for life, he somehow remained European. The European identities of Rudyard Kipling, George Santayana, and Vladimir Nabokov remain quite uncompromised by long years of residence in America. "*He* is an American," wrote Crèvecœur, answering his own question, "who, leaving behind him all his ancient prejudices and manners, receives new ones from the new mode of life he has embraced."[7] The key word is "embraced." Europeans here quoted normally observed with detachment or disdain rather than embraced with enthusiasm. The voluntary emigrant with intent of naturalization, a sort of cultural defector, might hope to qualify under Crèvecœur's definition. If he succeeded in doing so he would thereby disqualify himself as one of our witnesses. Crèvecœur was, unknown to himself, proposing an anthropological definition of national identity. Substitute for his words "prejudices and manners" a word unknown to him in this sense, the term "culture," and you have an anthropological concept. The "great metamorphosis" that Crèvecœur ascribes to a European's Americanization, in his words, "extinguishes all his European prejudices." Such a meta-

[5] Denis Donohue, "John Butler Yeats," in Marc Pachter, ed., *Abroad in America: Visitors to the New Nation, 1776–1914* (Washington, D.C., 1976), 261.
[6] Geoffrey Gorer, *The American People: A Study in National Character* (New York, revised ed., 1964), 31, 46.
[7] Crèvecœur, *Letters from an American Farmer*, 43.

morphosis rarely took place. Barring a few exceptions, and whatever their professed intentions, declared allegiance, or legal status, Europeans in America whose opinions we quote here remained predominantly European in the cultural or anthropological sense.

The American counterpart of these Europeans—the exile or expatriate in Europe—though a rarer phenomenon, was subject to the same anthropological principles. Again, with a few exceptions, the American abroad remained American, and often the longer he stayed the more American he became. The most famous instance was Benjamin Franklin, whose legal allegiance was constantly at issue while he was in France, but whose American cultural identity he brilliantly dramatized. Seven years abroad certainly did not Europeanize James Fenimore Cooper, nor did comparable or longer periods of European residence have that effect upon Nathaniel Hawthorne, Mark Twain, or Ernest Hemingway. The outstanding exception was Henry James, who after more than forty years as expatriate became a British citizen. But even James swore to his brother William that he kept his bond with his native land foremost in mind.

Neither a Europeanized American nor an Americanized European came forth who appeared capable of closing the cultural gap or removing the cultural blinders on either side of the Atlantic. On the European side there continued to prevail the old reticence, love of privacy, habits of ambivalence and irony, and a skepticism that sometimes verged on pessimism. On the American side persisted a characteristic forthrightness and openness, a mistrust of privacy, and a headlong energy that proceeded on assumptions of optimism. Between the two existed for a long time cultural differences more formidable in some ways than those between any two West European countries, differences of greater importance than the political issues that are more often stressed.

A book under the title the present one bears might be

assumed to cover more subjects than we intend to treat. It may be true, as a learned and thoughtful writer has suggested, that, "After the advent of Christianity, no other event has brought about such a radical change in European thinking as the actual discovery of America."[8] There can be no doubt that the impact of the New World on Old World thinking later became profound in many fields and that the subject deserves extensive study. But as important and fascinating as that subject is, it is not *our* subject and we will have to put it aside.

Similarly a related subject that is also beyond our limits is the images and ideas of Europe that Americans have formed over the centuries. Once they ceased thinking of themselves as Europeans who lived abroad and began to think of themselves as a distinctive people, Americans set about inventing their Europe as surely as Europeans had invented their America. Their inventions were in some measure an assertion of identity by a negative definition, declaring what they were in terms of what they were not. Americans came to picture Europe as the bankrupt past, whose people were oppressed and degraded by tyranny in a society ridden by vice, privilege, and corruption. The Old World was thus the dark antithesis of the New World, America the land of the future, rich with peace, prosperity, and freedom and blessed with purity. Thomas Jefferson wished there were "an ocean of fire" between the two—when he was not busy gathering treasures in the Old World to enrich the New.[9]

Putting aside all such tempting distractions and confining the subject to declared limits, we still find ourselves faced with all or more than we can cope with. Thousands have joined in the European game of deploring, baiting, or praising America over the last two centuries. They came from all over, wrote in all moods, and voiced all political views from left to

[8] Germán Arciniegas, *America in Europe: A History of the New World in Reverse* (San Diego, 1975), 5.

[9] Cushing Strout, *The American Image of the Old World* (New York, 1963).

right. For all of them transatlantic visibility was poor. Relatively few are still worth serious attention, but it is not easy to choose those who are and to sample them fairly. They tend to influence and repeat each other and to perpetuate stereotypes. A student of early English fiction about America finds that "Even admirers of America could not escape the habit of referring to it as though it were in a barbarous state."[10]

Most of them disavowed all prejudice and claimed nothing but the best of intentions. "Prejudiced I am not," declared Charles Dickens, "and never have been, otherwise than in favor of the United States."[11] Yet he could at the same time write to a friend in England, "I would not condemn you to a year's residence in this side of the Atlantic for any money."[12] Very few were as frank and forthright as Frances Trollope. Writing of "the population generally," Americans rich and poor, town and country, North and South, she said, "I do not like them. I do not like their principles, I do not like their manners, I do not like their opinions."[13] Frederick Marryat set out, he said to "do them justice, without praising them more than they deserve,"[14] but after publishing his book he admitted publicly, "My object was to do injury to democracy. . . . I wrote the book with this object, and wrote it accordingly."[15]

They wrote with varied objectives and purposes and with various classes of readers in mind. Most of them hoped for readers in America, but it seems evident that the audience most significant for them was the one back home, and the ideas, causes, and movements there that they wished to

[10] Robert B. Heilman, *America in English Fiction, 1760–1800* (Baton Rouge, 1937), 339.
[11] Charles Dickens, *American Notes* (Gloucester, Mass., 1968; original ed., 1842), 14.
[12] In Christopher Lasch's introduction to *American Notes*, cited above, p. x.
[13] Frances Trollope, *Domestic Manners of the Americans*, ed. Donald Smalley (New York, 1949; original ed., 1832), 404.
[14] Frederick Marryat, *A Diary in America, With Remarks on Its Institutions*, ed. Sydney Jackman (New York, 1962; original ed., 1839), xvi–xvii.
[15] Quoted in John Graham Brooks, *As Others See Us* (New York, 1908), 28.

promote or discourage. They wrote in different periods with political moods and interests in constant flux, and they wrote about an America that was changing all the time, changing far more rapidly than Europe and faster than generalizations were made about America. These circumstances, prevailing on both sides of the Atlantic throughout the period treated, make any generalization about European views of America and the value of them quite hazardous. This did not ever seem to keep Americans or Europeans from making them, however. In doing so their tendency was to be influenced strongly by the state of Euro-American harmony or lack of it prevailing at the time the generalizations were made.

Back in 1825 the American writer James K. Paulding published his *John Bull in America; or The New Munchausen*, a furious satire on foreign books about America. Harmony was hardly the word to describe relations between most English visitors and America at the time, and Paulding's satire faithfully reflected the fact. His protagonist leaves England determined, he said, "to look on the favorable side of the subject on all occasions . . . as free from prejudice . . . as any English traveler who ever visited the country," and feeling only the "sort of compassion . . . we feel for condemned criminals." His only surprise was "that a country like this, destitute of every virtue, and devoid of every attraction under heaven, should have lured from all parts of Christendom, crowds of emigrants, who . . . have sought misery and disappointment in these barbarous wilds."[16]

Forty years later the American Civil War had divided European sympathies and opinions, and even though foreign commentary remained predominantly negative, favorable views had become more prevalent. This was reflected in a book on the subject by the American poet and critic Henry Theodore Tuckerman published in 1864. It was by that time,

[16] James K. Paulding, *John Bull in America; or The New Munchausen* (New York, 1825), 1–2, 143–44.

he wrote, quite possible to find among our European critics "every degree of sympathy and antipathy, of refinement and vulgarity, of philosophical insight and shallow impertinence, from coarse malice to dull good nature, and from genial sense to repulsive bigotry."[17] Tuckerman provided his reader with generous samples of European antipathy, malice, and bigotry toward the New World up to his time.

That was at the end of the Civil War. At the end of the Second World War, Western Europeans felt beholden to America not only for military aid but for helping to rescue them from their postwar plight with the Marshall Plan. In that mood even some of our more hardened critics mellowed a bit and the more favorably inclined bestowed lavish praise. Henry Luce had predicted an "American Century" and Wendell Willkie had boasted of "a gigantic reservoir of good will toward us" the world around. Surveying foreign critics since the eighteenth century in preparing his anthology of their writings in 1947, Henry Steele Commager declared that "It all added up to a flattering picture." True, there had been a good deal of negative criticism over the years, but in his opinion, "jaundiced criticism came from the second-rate commentators rather than from the magisterial ones. The most judicious, the most learned, the most perspicacious, the most profound interpreters of America returned a verdict that ranged from sympathy to enthusiasm." He therefore felt justified in excluding from his anthology "the vulgarity, the impertinence, the malice, the bigotry, and I trust, the dullness" of the less judicious, learned and perspicacious, who were not so enthusiastic about America.[18]

The anthologist of the 1940s could hardly have anticipated the problems that revisions of his collection might entail in the decade that followed and later. For the 1950s brought

---

[17] Henry Theodore Tuckerman, *America and Her Commentators: With a Critical Sketch of Travel in the United States* (New York, 1864), especially pp. 252–92.

[18] Henry Steele Commager, *America in Perspective: The United States Through Foreign Eyes* (New York, 1947), xx–xxi.

on a prolonged and quite *un*flattering barrage of criticism from both left and right. And during the McCarthyite assault on free speech and the Bill of Rights generally the European middle class joined the left and the right in the attack on America's reputation as world leader of democratic nations. The attack included some of the bitterest anti-American criticism in the long history of the phenomenon, and it did not come exclusively from the vulgar, the fanatical, or the unlearned. In fact, intellectuals and academics were prominent in the anti-Americanism of left, right, and center opinion in Europe throughout this period. Americans in residence in Britain or on the Continent in those years felt it most keenly, but it did not escape attention at home. America was regularly denounced in the United Nations, and it came near being the scapegoat for the world's ills. In his Nobel Prize lecture in 1976, Saul Bellow complained that, "Every year we see scores of books and articles that tell the Americans what a state they are in—that make intelligent or simpleminded or extravagant or lurid or demented statements. All reflect the crises we are in while telling us what we must do about them; these analysts are produced by the very disorder and confusion they prescribe for."[19]

At least one other major shift in the balance of European opinion on America has occurred since the one that began in the 1950s. That coincided with the recent global outburst of pro-democratic sentiment. It broke forth almost simultaneously in the several European upheavals of 1989, and others before and after, in Latin America, Africa and Asia. To be pro-democratic, of course, is not necessarily to be pro-American. As we have seen, the term "democracy" is often put to strange uses. And even when endowed with more or less the meaning we give it in America, it can coexist abroad with ambivalent sentiment regarding its most prominent transatlantic manifestation. Even so, and despite these reserva-

[19] Saul Bellow, "The Nobel Lecture," *American Scholar* (Summer 1977), 319.

tions, it can hardly be doubted that the global shrinkage in the prestige of authoritarian doctrine about the path to man's political salvation and the decline of faith in dictatorial alternatives to democracy can hardly fail to improve the image of the oldest surviving democracy. At least the confessed failure of democracy's chief rivals took the wind out of the sails of some anti-American critics, emboldened the more friendly ones, and temporarily, at least, tipped the balance of foreign opinion to the American side. These changes are so recent that the new attitudes have scarcely had time to find voice and receive expression. Enough have been heard, however, to portend more to come.

Before we respond by proclaiming a new "American Century" and celebrate the recovery of a "reservoir of good will," I think it would be well to recall how transitory these cycles of foreign opinion have proved to be in the past, and how quickly one extreme has been followed by its opposite. In the instance at hand, for example, the very world changes that have so recently altered old-style anti-Americanism in Europe have at the same time heralded a new political and economic world order, or disorder, to come, and that in the immediate future. This includes the disintegration of the old Stalinist empire and the coming integration of a new colossus of Western Europe to be economically united in 1992. As the 500 million people of the eastern nations fly apart, the 320 millions of the western nations simultaneously begin to draw together to form what will probably be the greatest concentration of economic power in the world.

These are changes of a dimension that beggars the old clichés such as "turning point" and "watershed." They would appear to be the sort that can best be described as one of the hinges of history on which one age turns to another. America has been a bemused spectator rather than an active agent in these latter-day changes, and still seems undecided what to make of them—how much to welcome and how much to deplore. While she watches, the Old World is in many ways becoming a new world. One consequence will be that a new Old World will view an old New World with new eyes and from a different perspective. The probability is that in the foreseeable future another major shift will take place in the cycles of European views of America.

The present time would therefore seem to be a singularly opportune one in which to explore the history of the Old World's views of the New World. We will undertake to discover some clues about how those views have been shaped, how widely they have been shared, how long their cycles have run, and what has contributed to their change. By this means we might hope to be better prepared for other changes we may expect now to face and those soon to come than we have been for the many that have occurred in the past.

And what of the Europeans, whose criticisms Americans have endured for these centuries? For all the doubts, misgivings, and disdain of their intellectuals, for all the patronizing slurs and cool contempt of their aristocrats, and for all the anti-American bigotry of their left-wing and right-wing radicals, the Europeans have continued to emigrate and eagerly cast their lot with the benighted Americans, many millions in the nineteenth century and many more in the twentieth. And still they come, and more and more. And Americans of the present, save those of Asian or African origins, are made up of their descendants to the first, second, third, and more generations. So the people whose illusions and misguided opinions of us that we will be talking about are our ancestors or contemporary cousins.

THE OLD WORLD'S NEW WORLD

1

How It All Started

To BEGIN THE HISTORY of almost anything is to admit that
one is not really beginning at the beginning, that things
happened before one's starting point that are of importance to
what happened later in the part of the story to be told. This is
amply illustrated by the story that follows. The part of the story
I propose to tell about the Old World's ideas of the New World
only begins about a couple of centuries ago. Yet here we are
now on the eve of celebrating the five hundredth anniversary
of the most famous discovery of the New World by Europeans.

   To acknowledge the omission of three centuries, however, is not all that is due. My story includes—indeed it tends
to stress—the Old World's dreams, fantasies, imaginings,
hopes, and yearnings about the New World. And those began
even before 1492. Accounts of them occur in charming
legends and fiction of pre-Columbian discoveries of westward-
lying islands. They were pictured as idyllic, as the earthly
paradise of a golden age—all the Old World yearned for and
lacked. These dreams were not banished by the age of discovery but, with some variation, were applied throughout the
sixteenth century and later to the world that Columbus and his

successors discovered and explored and claimed as possessions for ambitious monarchs of the Old World. European lust for power, however, did not end European dreams of freedom. "For if America nurtured Europe's ambitions," observes J. H. Elliott, the historian of their encounter, "it also kept its dreams alive. And perhaps dreams were always more important than realities in the relationship of the Old World and the New."[1] Europeans continued to think of the New World as places "where men do not die unless they want to, where it is always summer, where food is plentiful, and where nobody works," a land with a magic that "turned naked Indians into gods and goddesses, warriors and nymphs, and what had risen out of a dream of antiquity became a mode of picturing actuality."[2]

Poets in the age of exploration could give the New World metaphoric uses of explicitly sexual character. One example is John Donne's "Going to Bed." Bidding his mistress ungirdle, disrobe, and license his hands for full exploration, he exclaims, "O my America! my new-found-land, / My king-dome, safeliest when with one man man'd, / My Myne of precious stone, My Emperie, / How blest am I in this discovering thee!" Such visions of bliss and felicity lent themselves readily to utopian uses as well. Two famous examples are Thomas More's *Utopia*, first published in 1516, and Francis Bacon's *New Atlantis*, published posthumously in 1627. Both of their imaginary islands were located in the New World.

The idyllic image, however, had a reverse side that was less attractive. The Golden Age was also an age of gold, gold and greed, that pitted Europeans against each other as well as against Indians. And the Indians came to be perceived as treacherous enemies and as savages who practiced human sacrifice, cannibalism, and the cruelest of tortures. They were clearly "children of the devil," "offspring of Satan." Theirs

[1] J. H. Elliott, *The Old World and the New*, 1492–1650 (Cambridge, Mass., 1970), 104.

[2] Howard Mumford Jones, *O Strange New World. American Culture: The Formative Years* (New York, 1964), 33.

was a land "filled with monsters animal and monsters human; it was a region of terrifying natural forces, of gigantic catastrophes, of unbearable heat and cold. . . ." In its formative years and beyond the European image of the New World was very much a Renaissance creation. In part that meant an image of derring-do, of pageantry, splendor, and ceremony. It was also the age of the Borgias and Machiavelli as well as of Castiglione, a fiercely competitive world of conquest, violence, and cruelty, of cunning, conspiracy, treachery, and blood-drenched ruthlessness. In the Old World coinage of New World images in the sixteenth and seventeenth centuries there were always two sides.[3]

The coins of the eighteenth century had new images, but the two sides contrasted as sharply as ever: "the eulogy and slander, the panegyric and vituperation," as Antonello Gerbi puts it in his remarkable work, *The Dispute of the New World*.[4] The "Dispute" he pursues with such tenacity and patience often grows onerous and obtuse, and the adversaries become incredibly vain and abusive of one another, capable of ignoring incontrovertible evidence in order to advance their arguments and demean their opponents. Dr. Gerbi takes it all in his stride: "So the admirer and the slanderer of the savage find themselves for once in perfect agreement, in their mutual scorn of the humble facts."[5] His humor and his droll wit never fail him, and he carries his erudition with grace.

Gerbi's *Dispute of the New World* begins in the middle of the eighteenth century with one of the most celebrated scientists (and accomplished egotists) of the Enlightenment, Comte de Buffon. A member of the French Academy and virtually all the learned European societies of his time, Buffon spoke with

---

[3] Ibid., 70, 127–31.

[4] Antonello Gerbi, *The Dispute of the New World: The History of a Polemic, 1750–1900.* (Revised and Enlarged Edition translated by Jeremy Moyle, New York, 1973. Originally published in Milan, 1955, as *La disputa del Nuovo Mondo: Storia de una polemica, 1750–1900*), xi.

[5] Ibid.

authority and assurance about the "melancholy regions" of the New World (which he never visited). These lands emerged from *le deluge* of Biblical times later than the rest of the world. Being thus "overloaded with humid and noxious vapors," they could "afford nourishment only to cold men and feeble animals" or to "insects, reptiles, and all animals which wallow in the mire." The tapir of Brazil provoked his ridicule as "this elephant of the New World" and the llama was more ridiculous as the best it could do for a camel. The largest American animals were one-fourth to one-tenth the size of their counterparts in the Old World.[6] Domestic animals imported from Europe shrank and dwindled to dwarfish caricatures of the original stock. The male of the native human species is "feeble and small in his organs of generation; he has neither body hair nor beard, and no ardor for the female of his kind . . . he lacks vivacity, and is lifeless in his soul."[7]

Buffon was succeeded and surpassed as degrader of the New World by Abbé Cornelius de Pauw, an Alsatian by birth. In his *Recherches philosophiques sur les Americains,* two volumes published in Berlin in 1768–69, the abbé achieved the climax of vehemence in the Buffonian style of anti-American rhetoric. He declared the New World unfit for human habitation, "so ill-favored by nature that all it contains is either degenerate or monstrous." There "the earth, full of putrefaction, was flooded with lizards, snakes, serpents, reptiles and insects." He was "certain that the conquest of the New World . . . has been the greatest of all misfortunes to befall mankind." It is no wonder that, to Gerbi, "It is obvious that de Pauw is much more radical than Buffon." Granting that de Pauw was provoked by fantastic claims of defenders of America and the Noble Savage, Gerbi continues: "But the impetuous de Pauw gets carried away by his rebuttal, generalizing

[6] Ibid., 3–7, 56–58.
[7] Henry Steele Commager and Elmo Giordanelli, *Was America a Mistake? An Eighteenth Century Controversy* (Columbia, S.C., 1967), 57–64.

unashamedly and maintaining seriously that in the American climate many animals lose their tails, dogs lose their bark, the meat of the ox becomes tough, and the genitals of the camel cease to function. . . . He tells of savages with pyramidal or conical craniums, and of Americans . . . with square or cubic heads."[8]

It is difficult in our day to understand how such outrageous views as those of de Pauw could have been taken seriously by his Enlightenment contemporaries, much less by their posterity. But we are presented with ample evidence that his theories "rapidly produced an angry swarm of replies and counterreplies"—both pro and con, defense and attack. The abbot's critics rallied to defend the Noble Savage, Virgin Nature, Progress, and the civilizing mission of Christianity and mobilized their forces to beat back this pessimistic view of history and its slander of the New World. Savants taking de Pauw's side stoutly maintained that the conquest of America by Europe was a curse to both worlds. To America it brought disease, slavery, and destruction, to Europe inflation, wars, and death for millions. America was pictured as a vast misfortune, a colossal "mistake."[9]

Many writers participated in the dispute over the New World, but the writings of Abbé de Pauw remained the chief point of departure and provocation to the end of the century and beyond. Savants paired off, pro and con. The famous Abbé Guilliaume Thomas François Raynal sided with his fellow abbot, while Dom Antoine-Joseph Pernety, protégé of Frederick the Great, and Fillipo Mazzei, friend of Thomas Jefferson, championed the New World. If Dr. Johnson scorned all "cant in defense of Savages," Horace Walpole predicted that "The next Augustan age will dawn on the other side of the Atlantic." In de Pauwian style, Immanuel Kant declared: "The American people are incapable of civiliza-

---

[8] Gerbi, *The Dispute*, 53, 56–67.
[9] Ibid., 80.

tion," while Johann Gottfried Herder professed his fond and admiring affinity for all American people. Among the romantic poets, Keats once pronounced America "that most hateful land," while Byron, Shelley, and Goethe wrote in various optimistic and hopeful ways about the New World: "*Amerika, du hast es besser.*"[10]

According to Dr. Gerbi the European dispute about the New World that had so enthralled his imagination "reaches its peak in the antithesis between Humboldt and Hegel, and at the same time the point of widest divergence between the two extremes." At the one extreme was "the antiquated arbitrariness" of the Swabian philosopher Hegel who "dialectalizes and polarizes everything" including the two hemispheres along with all their inhabitants and contents. In order to satisfy his "immensely powerful yearning for a single explanation for the infinite diversity of the world," Hegel embraced the theories of Buffon and de Pauw and carried them to greater extremes. Hegel encountered his opposite number in the naturalist Alexander von Humboldt of Prussia, who actually went to America in 1799, in part to test out Buffonian and de Pauwian theories. He returned with ample refutation of them along with a great enthusiasm for the opulence, diversity, and natural wonders of the New World. Thereafter he lost no opportunity for airing his disagreement with Buffon and de Pauw and pouring no little scorn and urbane ridicule on Hegel.[11]

"In the decades that follow," writes Gerbi, "all American enthusiasts rely on the vigorous assertions of the Prussian naturalist, and all its slanderers take comfort in the pronouncements of the Swabian philosopher. There are almost no new developments." Of course Europeans continued to argue about America endlessly, especially about the United

[10] Ibid., 173, 286, 330, 359–72; Commager and Giordanelli, *Was America a Mistake?*, 100–102, 135–36.
[11] Gerbi, *The Dispute*, 406–18.

States, and "hundreds of travelers and archaeologists became deservedly famous" for their pronouncements on the subject. Among them he mentions and discusses Tocqueville, Schopenhauer, Comte, Stendhal, Carlyle, the Trollopes, Dickens, and many others. But after Hegel and Humboldt "the dispute could not have and did not have any further developments of interest." Many joined in the colloquy, some of them quite famous, but they had changed the subject from "the physical nature of the continent to the society formed therein." And, alas, "the name of de Pauw falls into the most complete oblivion."

It was almost as if he resented his chain of thought being rudely interrupted by an irrelevancy. So long and so deeply had the learned Italian scholar been absorbed in the quarrels of de Pauw that after his eclipse the European arguments about the New World did not have "any further developments of interest"—at least not for him. He summarily placed such developments and their perpetrators in a final chapter, "more in the way of an appendix" (a mere 122 pages), to which he gave the title, "The Dispute's Trivialization and Obstinate Vitality."[12]

What the nineteenth- and twentieth-century disputes about America had to add to the eighteenth-century disputes inspired by Buffon and de Pauw was indeed trivial or negligible. The leading figures and their arguments were all but forgotten. The savants of the Enlightenment were, after all, arguing mainly about questions of geology, flora, fauna, and aborigines, matters that later disputants gladly left to scientists of appropriate disciplines. Post-Enlightenment disputes were not about native Americans and their environment but about European-Americans and their society, institutions, and culture—about what was happening to Old World standards, values, and ideals in the New World, about whether America and its economy and its democracy might prove a menace or a

12 Ibid., 417, 442–564.

model for Europe. These questions may have trivialized the Enlightenment dispute or ignored it, but they seemed more important to Europeans and Americans of a later time.

It would be ungrateful, however, not to say churlish, for us to dismiss the erudite findings of our historian of ideas as quaint, antiquated, or irrelevant. In acknowledging the shift of European interest and criticism from the nature of the continent to the nature of its society, he shrewdly observes: "A change of target, but not always of method and arguments. In fact the verdict pronounced on the new American nations and their 'civilization' often takes on the tone and coloring of the diatribes on the animals and natives," diatribes that perpetuated such absurdities in the eighteenth-century dispute. Science may have redeemed soil and skies, flora and fauna of the New World, but "its people and states were still measured with the yardstick of simplistic comparisons, contests of merit, polarizing parallels."[13]

In addition to the shift in the period of time covered, the account that follows makes other departures. Some of these changes expand, but more of them contract and curtail the field and subjects considered by eighteenth-century savants. For them the New World included the whole hemisphere, insular as well as continental, South as well as North America, and speculation sometimes focused on the southern and Latin half, with special attention to tropical and subtropical parts. My attention shifts northward to Anglo-America and all but exclusive concern with the United States. The timespan is also contracted to the centuries after the winning of independence. During the earlier period, curiosity was directed largely to the New World's natural wonders and differences, while in later times European interest has centered upon human peculiarities and institutions. On the highest levels these interests are illustrated by the works of Humboldt on the one hand and those of Tocqueville on the other: while the former had little

[13] Ibid., 443.

to say about human institutions, the latter was absorbed less by natural wonders than by wonders human.

The Dispute of the New World is a history of ideas in the traditional sense: how ideas originated, who supported them, whom they stimulated, challenged and provoked, and the response of supporters and opponents. In the study that follows the emphasis is on the European responses not to each other or to some formal thesis, but to events and developments in America and their significance for comparable events in Europe. European responses to such events and developments may involve them in disputes with those of opposing views, but it is not the resulting polemics and the rivalries of the participants that matter so much as the views themselves and the American conditions that provoked such a great variety of ideas about America and such distortions of American realities.

I have arbitrarily limited the American response to Europeans, almost to the point of exclusion, with a very few exceptions. The chief exception is Thomas Jefferson. The reason for introducing his views at this point is that his response is directed at the errors and defamations of Enlightenment savants Buffon, Raynal, dePauw and company, whose views have been aired above.

In his *Notes on the State of Virginia* Jefferson devoted many pages and several elaborate tables of evidence he had collected to refute the charges of American inferiority made by Buffon and Raynal. [14] Arriving in France as American minister in 1785 and eager to beard the savants, he sent his friend the Marquis de Chastellux to Buffon with a privately printed copy of his *Notes* and the gift of a large panther's skin. This led to an invitation to dine with Buffon in the *Jardin du Roi* and to further exchanges, in which Jefferson believed he had persuaded the Count of the error of his ways. With so many European slanders and aspersions to correct, the Virginian

[14] Thomas Jefferson, *Notes on the State of Virginia* (London, 1787), 64–122.

enlisted help from friends in America. One of them organized a hunting party of twenty men to collect the skin, horns and skeleton of a moose, and horns of the caribou, elk, deer, and spike horned buck. These were dispatched in a large box to Paris at great expense to help Mr. Jefferson confound the stupid Europeans. [15]

As for the alleged dwarfishness of New World animals, the Count had not only horns and hides of existing species, but Jefferson's word for the existence of the skeleton of a presumably extinct American mammoth that "bespeaks an animal of five or six times the cubic volume of the elephant, as Mons. de Buffon has admitted." Whether wild or domestic, native or imported, he declared, New World animals held their own or exceeded in size those of the Old. The same held true, so the American minister stoutly maintained, of the human species of the New World, whether native or those of European ancestry. The Virginian gave eloquent account of his experiences with Indians when he was a child and when he was governor of his state. [16]

When he took up the charge that life in America enfeebled Europeans as well as Indians, Jefferson was careful to exempt Buffon from endorsing that error. That was the peculiar distinction of Abbé Raynal, and Jefferson came down hard on the abbé, though not in his book. He delighted in relating elsewhere the story of a party given by Franklin in Paris. Raynal was holding forth on his theory of human degeneration in the New World, when Franklin asked his French guests to rise, then his American guests. It happened that the latter were "of the finest stature and form; while those on the other side were remarkably diminutive, and the abbé himself, was a mere shrimp." Jefferson was even more severe, pri-

---

[15] Jefferson's Notes presented by the author to Buffon was one of 200 copies privately printed in Paris in 1782. The first public edition is the one cited above. Dumas Malone, Jefferson and His Time (6 vols., Boston, 1948–81), II, 93–94, 99–100.

[16] Jefferson, Notes on Virginia, 67, 72, 91, 94; Malone, Jefferson and His Time, II, 98–102.

vately, in his strictures upon the volumes on America by de Pauw: "a compiler from the works of others; and of the most unlucky description; for he seems to have read the writings of travellers, only to collect and republish their lies. It is really remarkable, that in the three volumes 12 mo. of small print, it is scarcely possible to find one truth."[17]

When challenged to name "one good poet" produced by America, Jefferson asked how long the Greeks existed as a people "before they produced a Homer, the Romans a Virgil, the French a Racine and Voltaire, the English a Shakespeare and Milton." The Americans, he reminded them, had less than a decade of independence and fewer than three million population. Given their advantage in centuries of history and millions of inhabitants, it seemed "as unjust as it is unkind" of European critics to ask if his countrymen had produced "one man of genius in a single art or a single science." Especially so when, "In war we have produced a Washington, whose memory will be adored while liberty shall have votaries," not to mention "a Franklin, than whom no one of the present age has made more important discoveries" in physics, or a "Rittenhouse second to no astronomer living." To do so well, in view of its much larger population, "France then should have half a dozen in each of these lines, and Great Britain half that number, equally eminent." In view of this evidence the author of the Declaration of Independence declared of his fledgling nation that "We therefore have reason to believe she can produce her full quotas of genius."[18]

Perhaps the samples so far adduced adequately illustrate the tone and temper of the eighteenth-century dispute, the arrogance and ignorance of the European critics as well as the

---

[17] Gilbert Chinard, "Eighteenth Century Theories on America As a Human Habitat," *Proceedings of the American Philosophical Society* IXC (1947): 16. In this article Chinard also rounds up responses to European theories by John Adams, Benjamin Franklin, David Rittenhouse, Benjamin Rush, and other Americans of their time.

[18] Ibid., 43.

outrage and indignation of New World defenders. The single sample of American response offered might suffice to suggest why it seemed advisable to limit the outpourings of the patriots. Even a spokesman of the stature and dignity of the great Virginian could stretch a point in a pinch. I have refrained from mentioning his American moose so tall that reindeer could walk underneath its belly, or his suggestion that mammoths of the sort whose fossils dwarfed elephants might still roam northern wilds of the New World. With such as that from the Sage of Monticello, we scarcely need the flag waving of a Whitman and his raptures over "the continent of glories," and the "splendid race" of Americans with their "majestic faces, clear eyes, and perfect physique."[19]

If it served no better purpose than to satisfy idle curiosity or a taste for the recondite, or merely to suggest what preceded the period studied here, it would not be possible to justify the attention I have asked for the quarrels of the eighteenth-century dispute. But it can usefully serve as an introduction to the chapters that follow. Readers will find more than a few similarities between the disputes over America among be-wigged and powdered Europeans of an earlier time and those of a later day with which I will be concerned here. No conical or pyramidal-headed Americans turn up in the European accounts of more recent times, but their pages contain numerous blockheads and knuckleheads. The newer monstrosities are those of mind and spirit rather than those of body and frame. They are perceived as degenerations or deformities of a cultural rather than a biological or physical character. But the parade of grotesqueries and travesties, though wearing different masks and costumes, is about as colorful in one period as in the other. Among the latter-day European detractors and slanderers, America is still a "mistake," though one of man's rather than of God's or nature's making.

<hr />

[19] Jefferson, *Notes on Virginia*, 106–10; Whitman, "Thoughts," *Leaves of Grass*, in *Walt Whitman: Complete Poetry and Collected Prose* (New York, 1982), 601–2.

Among latter-day European supporters of America, on the other hand, their enthusiasms are often inspired by what they perceive as the progress or realization in the New World of dreams, ideas, political systems, and economic plans they are seeking to promote at home. The idealized visions of the transatlantic world they conjure up are thus often inspired by hopes, aspirations, and crusades for the future of Europe. If the New World embodied the hopes and dreams of the Old World among pro-Americans, it supplied anti-Americans with the incarnation, often the exaggeration, of indigneous evils of materialism, greed, and alienation firmly rooted in their own social order. Differences over their polemical uses of the American symbol brought anti-Americans and pro-Americans into head-on conflict that was often as furious and irrational as that in the bygone era of de Pauwians and anti-de Pauwians.

2

The Silver Screen
in the West

EVEN BEFORE THE EIGHTEENTH-CENTURY THEORY of degeneration and depravity in America had reached full expression, it collided headlong with a quite different vision, indeed its very opposite. This was eventually to flower as romantic Europe's America, the American "Mirage," it has been called. It borrowed from Rousseau's pastoral idyl of virtue and agrarian felicity as well as from the fantasies of two revolutions. The romantics idealized America as uncritically as the theorists of degeneration had denigrated it. In a letter on the Americans to Dr. Richard Price in 1778, Turgot wrote, "They are the hope of the human race; they may well become its model." But the full perfection of the mirage arrived later, overlapping the last years of the old regime and the worst years of Terror in the French Revolution. That period saw what has been described as the first flowering of modern secular mysticism, the hope of man's creating an earthly heaven and the faith in his ability to realize his dream.[1]

[1] Durand Echeverria, *Mirage in the West: A History of the French Image of American Society to 1815* (Princeton, 1951), 116.

In those euphoric years America served as symbol of things hoped for and model of what faith could do. The faithful poured forth apostrophes of praise and admiration. What they wrote about America has to be seen to be believed. Hector St. John de Crèvecœur, the Americanized Frenchman, pronounced his temporarily adopted country in 1782 simply "the most perfect society now existing in the world." Any immigrant, he declared, "voluntarily loves a country where everything is so lovely," and he found it impossible to "describe the various emotions of love, of gratitude, of conscious pride, which thrill my heart and often overflow in involuntary tears."[2] His friend Brissot de Warville, a future leader of the French Revolution, described his arrival in Boston in 1788: "How joyfully, my dear friend, did I leap ashore to tread this land of liberty! . . . A refugee from despotism, I was at last to have the happiness of witnessing freedom. . . ."[3] Brissot's compatriot, the Marquis de Barbé-Marbois illustrates the theme of pastoral tranquility by his description of a scene of rural happiness: "our imaginations," he wrote, "were transported into the vales of Arcady. It was the image of innocence and peace, and if I have ever believed in happiness, I did so then."[4]

In frustration over their own troubles, Europeans of the period often contrasted the freedom and happiness of America with despair at home. Thus Julian Niemcewicz, a Polish companion of Thaddeus Kosciuszko during his American visit in 1797, declared that freedom was something "only Americans in the whole world have the right to celebrate," while Europeans "are all crushed whether by chains at home or by

[2] Hector St. John de Crèvecœur, *Letters from an American Farmer* (London, 1912), 24, 41, 57.

[3] Brissot de Warville, *New Travels in the United States of America, 1788,* tr. Mara Soreanu Vamos and Durand Echeverria, ed. Echeverria (Cambridge, Mass., 1964), 84.

[4] François, Marquis de Barbé-Marbois, *Our Revolutionary Forefathers. The Letters During His Residence in the United States as Secretary of the French Legation,* 1779–1785 (New York, 1929), 91–92.

foreign bonds; from the Tiber to the Volga people groan in fetters."[5] European pilgrims to America struck classical poses and sought the noble simplicity of the Roman Republic. Thus Vicomte de Chateaubriand described himself as, "full of enthusiasm for the ancients, a Cato seeking everywhere for the rigidity of early Roman manners."[6] They often reported their findings negatively in joyful catalogues of things not found. "Here are no aristocratical families, no courts, no kings, no bishops, no ecclesiastical dominion . . . no great refinements of luxury," boasted Crèvecœur.[7] If Barbé-Marbois found himself a sightseeing tourist without sights to see—no "Titian, or Raphael, or Correggio, or Poussin," indeed "no crowns, no robes of ancient kings, no tomb of some ancient poet"—he rejoiced nevertheless to find "no tolls on each bridge, no seignorial rights . . . no salt tax . . . no monopoly . . . no smugglers . . . no farm guards."[8] These were the chains of the past, evils left behind in Europe.

America of the Mirage was the best of all possible worlds—a new start for mankind and a revival of antique virtue, a model for revolution and a return to nature, a golden age of present, past, and future. The usual pilgrimage to Monticello and an evening with the Sage seemed to confirm all this—or so the pilgrims regularly reported in their memoirs.

Then very quickly the Mirage began to fade. For the French, with their own revolution as dream generator and justifier, it became superfluous, and for opponents of their revolution it was repugnant. The Terror and then the Counter-revolution sent waves of refugees—among them Talleyrand, Raynal, the duc d'Orleans, future king of the

[5] Julian Ursyn Niemcewicz, *Under Their Vine and Fig Tree. Travels Through America in 1797–1799, 1805, with some Further Account of Life in New Jersey* (Elizabeth, N.J., 1965), 128.

[6] *Chateaubriand's Travels in America*, tr. Richard Switzer (Lexington, Ky., 1969), 15.

[7] Crèvecœur, *Letters from an American Farmer*, 40.

[8] Barbé-Marbois, *Our Revolutionary Forefathers*, 85–86, 88–89.

French, and the duc de La Rochefoucauld-Liancourt—who saw America with different eyes. Landing in Philadelphia in 1794, Talleyrand wrote, "My mind was totally indifferent to the novelties which, as a rule, excite the interest of travellers." American vulgarity, materialism, and lack of refinement repelled him.[9] The more sympathetic La Rochefoucauld also deplored "an immoderate love of money, hardness of heart," even though he considered Americans "on the whole a good people."[10] Opinions varied widely, but they no longer included idealization of America and they did include more and more disenchantment, cynicism, and outbursts of contempt. Even the old theory of New World degeneration was revived and America was once more pronounced a mistake. Political quarrels eventuating in an undeclared war further alienated Franco-American relations and diminished French interest. In a remarkably short space of time conservatives were to complete the dismantling of the Mirage and turn the work of idealization completely upside down, as they had done before.

When the French Revolution fell into disrepute for resort to terror, collapse of the republic, and submission to dictatorship, it was perhaps inevitable that conservatives and counter-revolutionaries should look to America for proof that they were right and for evidence of what went wrong. Where better might one find such proof than in the benighted transatlantic republic that still boasted of liberty and equality and the heresy of democracy. Populated by the refuse of the Old World, according to its conservative critics, America was a nation of bores. It was barren of the arts, doomed to mediocrity, denied all distinction and the finer things of life, and regarded as a footmat of condescension and contempt by conservatives and reactionaries throughout the Western World.

[9]*Memoirs of the Prince de Talleyrand*, ed. duc de Broglie, tr. Raphael Ledos de Beaufort (5 vols., London, 1891), I, 175, 181.

[10]François Alexander Frédéric, duc de La Rochefoucauld-Liancourt, *Travels Through the United States of North America* . . . (2 vols., London, 1799), I, 45; II, 657–58.

Alternating with these outbursts of scorn and contempt on the right that continued through the nineteenth and into the twentieth century were sunny spells of praise, admiration, and sympathy from those of the Old World who were then struggling for democracy. They continued to find in American democracy, despite its shortcomings, ample cause for enthusiasm and inspiration. Their support offset and to some extent counterbalanced the adverse propaganda of the right and continued to do so until, in the twentieth century, the conservative right was joined by the Marxist left as critics of American democracy.

While quite as astringent as the criticism of the old conservatives, that of the new radicals, coming from the opposite end of the political spectrum, was of course very different. Instead of holding up American democracy as the prime example of political evil wrought by rash defiance of authority and pretensions of equality, left wing radicals pictured it as world leader of reaction, foremost among capitalist oppressors, imperialist aggressors, and aggressive militarists. Between assaults from the right and attacks from the left, with intellectuals joining in from both sides, America came in for rather more than its share of opprobrious criticism from abroad.

If it has been made to appear that European conceptions of America were subject to wild swings from one extreme to the other, that appearance is not misleading. From America as mistake, as menace, as catastrophe, to America as dream, as salvation, as utopia would have to be termed a transmogrification—it calls for that big a word. And by the end of the eighteenth century a second reversal, quite as drastic, was in the making. In these respects that century was prologue to the centuries that followed. Only the opposites later tended more and more to coexist—defamation along with exaltation. Between the swings from fears to hopes that these extremes embodied there was little chance for moderation.

More than a century ago James Russell Lowell observed that "for some reason or other, the European has rarely been able to see America except in caricature."[11] Later on, Samuel Gompers was to remark that Europeans were given to viewing the transatlantic republic either in a convex or a concave mirror, but always distorted.[12] What Europeans for a time once thought they saw across the Atlantic in the eighteenth century has been aptly called the Mirage in the West. I would suggest for the long run of more than two centuries an admittedly anachronistic metaphor—the Silver Screen in the West. On it shifting pictures were projected not by the viewed but by the transatlantic viewers, and the images that appeared there tell us more about the European projectors than about the Americans they projected. Moreover the audience chiefly addressed was not in the New World but in the Old.

The pictures projected on the Screen by European conservatives in this period were predominantly British. Great Britain and America were poorly paired for this relationship: the most aristocratic society of the time as critic of the most democratic, rejected parent against rebellious offspring, sullen partners in ongoing family quarrels. Britain still bred pro-American radicals who would continue to be heard. But conservatives were in the saddle in the era of Napoleon and later.

After the collapse of the democratic experiment in France, the American Republic remained for a time the only state of any size in the world that still practiced and flaunted the heresies of democracy and equality. It clung to doctrines that conservatives held to be forever discredited by the French blood-bath and dictatorship and plunged recklessly onward through the depths of democratic degradation. The United States was a refuge for revolutionists, a center of subversion, a

---

[11] James Russell Lowell, "On a Certain Condescension in Foreigners," *Atlantic Monthly* XXIII (1869): 89.

[12] Henry Pelling, *America and the British Left from Bright to Bevan* (London, 1956), 161.

standing challenge to the establishment. It must be taught a lesson, exposed for its failures, pilloried for its horrors, and made an example—especially for those radicals at home who looked to the west for inspiration. The conservative critique was the work of many minds over a long period, but certain themes remained basic and fairly constant. [13]

Americans were democrats. Democracy was the root of most evils. Instead of more freedom it assured less. Its subjects lived in abject submission to the tyranny of the majority. They were without any means of redress that was not controlled by the majority. Press, pulpit, bench, and bar all bowed to the tyranny. Citizens trembled in a "torment of fear" before public opinion, which they worshiped as "the established religion." They were permitted less independence of mind and freedom of speech than the people of any European country and no longer even understood what such freedom meant. They were worse governed because they drove those best qualified to govern from politics and elected the least qualified and the corrupt. Trusting the whim of the mob, defying established wisdom, unrestrained by any aristocracy, church, or military, according to a Tory writer, the American democracy had proved that mankind was not yet able to govern itself. He added that in his opinion it never would.

Americans were equal. They worshiped equality above liberty, indeed above all things. Granted they raised the lower orders in some degree, they did so by lowering the whole culture and society to one dead level of mediocrity. They were all equal and all alike—alike in thought, in speech, in dress, expression, manner, in the very way they walked, the food they ate, and the gestures they made. All was uniformity, and all conformed. Uniformity assured the appearance of equal-

---

[13] The following views on American characteristics (pp. 20–22) are from British writers in the first half of the nineteenth century whose works are frequently cited later. Typical of them are Thomas Ashe (1808), William Foxx (1822), Basil Hall (1829), Frances Trollope (1832), Thomas Hamilton (1833), Frederick Marryat (1839), Charles Dickens (1842), Thomas C. Grattan (1809), Anthony Trollope (1862).

ity. Variety was rare, eccentricity unknown. Privacy was not respected and originality, distinction, and excellence in any department either did not exist or was carefully concealed. Most insufferable of all for the conservative observer were the pretensions of the lower orders. Newly landed immigrants acquired these pretensions almost instantly. Servants and social inferiors were often difficult to identify by appearance or manner. They showed no deference to their superiors and sometimes not even common courtesy. They were, in short, equal.

Americans pursued happiness. In fact they officially declared "the pursuit of happiness" a matter of national policy. Yet the pursuit appeared vain and unsuccessful. Theirs was a dull, morose, and melancholy society. They seemed to have no spirit of conviviality, little spontaneous sociability, and rarely any real sense of community. The prevailing dullness was unrelieved by gaiety or amusements, and rarely enlivened by music or laughter.

They were quiet Americans, silent to the point of sullenness, communicating in monosyllables among themselves, and among strangers not at all. Even in a barber shop a silence of nine minutes was clocked, broken only by a sneeze. At the hotel, table dining was a barbaric race set off by a tocsin. Food was seized, gobbled, bolted, wolfed with never a word of conversation or a gesture of courtesy and with the dispatch and voracity of dogs in a kennel. Drinking was also an antisocial act, done alone, standing up, again silently, without ceremony, and at a gulp.

Americans were materialists. They proclaimed the pursuit of happiness but they were obsessed with the pursuit of gain, material gain, dollars. Theirs was a work-work-work ethic that left them neither leisure nor capacity for the finer things of life. The civilization they were building produced little in scholarship, science, literature, or the arts that commanded notice in the rest of the world.

Such were the pictures the conservatives projected on the Silver Screen in the West. They put in a few lighter touches, of course, droll aspects, and comic relief, even some friendly if condescending concessions, and a few acknowledgments of improvement. But from the beginning through the ninth decade of the nineteenth century, the dour conservative view of the American scene predominated and held fairly constant. In 1888 Matthew Arnold summed up one aspect in observing "a want of the *interesting*" in American civilization as well as an absence of "elevation and beauty."[14] His contemporary, Sir Lepel Griffin, a Tory of strong views on the subject, rounded off the conservative consensus:

> America is the country of disillusion and disappoint-
> ment, in politics, literature, culture, and art, in its scenery, its
> cities, and its people. With some experience of every country
> in the civilized world, I can think of none except Russia in
> which I would not prefer to reside, in which life would not be
> more worth living, less sordid and mean and unlovely.[15]

In the meantime, through the same years, European opponents of the conservatives, the liberals, reformers, working-class leaders, radicals and revolutionaries, were projecting a very different drama of shadows and symbols on the Silver Screen. Sometimes these seemed the deliberately contrived opposites, the mirror images of the conservative pictures. "The manners of Americans (in America) are the best I ever saw," avowed Harriet Martineau;[16] and James S. Buckingham pronounced them "almost uniformly decorous, civil, obliging . . . quiet, orderly, and inoffensive."[17] Francis Grund, a recent immigrant from Bohemia, thought Ameri-

[14] Matthew Arnold, *Civilization in the United States*, 190.
[15] Lepel Griffin, *The Great Republic* (London, 1884), 2.
[16] Harriet Martineau, *Society in America* (3 vols., 1837; New York, 1966), III, 53–54.
[17] James Silk Buckingham, *The Slave States of America* (2 vols., London, 1842), I, 470.

can manners "as far removed from the elegance of courts, as they are from the boorishness of the lower classes in Europe; and perhaps, equally free from the vices of both." With "no time to cultivate fashionable elegance," Americans were "notwithstanding a highly sociable people."[18] Far from seeing them as gloomy, melancholy, and sullen, the Scottish traveler Alexander Mackay at mid-nineteenth century found them "frank, communicative, and not unfrequently mercurial in their dispositions."[19] Instead of the dullness of universal materialism, the Scottish visitor David Macrae began on landing "to feel a quickening of all the pulses of life. You not only find yourself able to work more, and work faster . . . you find yourself impelled to do it. Sensation is keener and more rapid. You live faster—live more within a given time." At this pace happiness was not merely pursued, it was overtaken, possessed, ravished.[20] By 1837 Martineau thought Americans already possessed "many things for which the rest of the civilised world is still struggling"; more important, they were "in possession of the glorious certainty that time and exertions will infallibly secure all wisely desired objects.[21]

Both radicals and conservatives cited Tocqueville's *Democracy in America* for their purposes. The very fact that each could do so places Tocqueville outside the categories of both, for he neither praised nor censured without qualification and was full of troublesome ambiguities. By temperament and instinct he was with the aristocrats and conservatives, but by drift of logic and conclusions he was often with the radicals. An exceptionally gifted and scrupulous intelligence, he has to be kept apart.

[18] Francis J. Grund, *The Americans in Their Moral, Social, and Political Relations* (Boston, 1837), 14–15.

[19] Alexander Mackay, *The Western World; Or Travels in the United States in 1846–47* . . . (2 vols., Philadelphia, 1849), II, 283.

[20] David Macrae, *The Americans at Home: Pen-and-Ink Sketches of American Men, Manners, and Institutions* (2 vols., Edinburgh, 1870), I, 17–18.

[21] Martineau, *Society in America*, III, 298.

The great American paradox that blurred all projections on the Silver Screen was the paradox of slavery in the home of freedom. Both conservatives and radicals condemned black slavery, though in different degrees and with different purposes. Strangely enough, neither side appeared much concerned with consequences following on emancipation. Indeed the great events of American history, even Civil War, Emancipation, and Reconstruction, made surprisingly little change in the projections of believers and nonbelievers.

The paeans of believers continued. "Truly I am grateful to this nation," declared the utopian Frances Wright, for it has "thawed my heart, and filled it with hopes which I had not thought I could know again."[22] I regard the American people as a great embryo poet," wrote Harriet Martineau, "now moody, now wild," but destined "to create something so magnificent as the world has scarcely begun to dream."[23] John Bright and Richard Cobden made America their prototype of a democratic utopia. "Was there ever in the history of the world a better government," asked Cobden rhetorically in 1848, and "can such intelligence, civilization and moral and material well-doing be elsewhere found?"[24] Bright assured his constituents in 1866 that the United States had "all the virtues which belong to the greatest nations on the face of the earth." These democratic and pro-American enthusiasms were a heritage of Chartism, shared by radical labor leaders, by their immigrant kinsmen across the Atlantic, and spread through the working class by a labor press full of eulogies of their views. British artisans were usually the staunchest European supporters of American institutions.[25]

[22] An Englishwoman [Frances Wright], *Views of Society and Manners in America; in a Series of Letters from That Country to a Friend in England, During the Years 1818, 1819, and 1820* (New York, 1821), 373.

[23] Martineau, *Society in America*, I, 39–40.

[24] Richard Cobden, *The American Diaries*, ed. Elizabeth H. Cowley (Princeton, 1952), 31; Frank Thistlethwaite, *Anglo-American Connections in the Early Nineteenth Century* (Philadelphia, 1959), 43.

[25] Pelling, *America and the British Left*, 16–17, 28–29.

The continental countries had their own believers, especially vocal among the Scandinavian peoples. The Norwegian
Ole Munch Raeder pronounced the country in the 1840s
"without equal either in the past or the present" for its peace
and prosperity.[26] His compatriot Fredrika Bremer, seeking for
"one expression which would portray the people of the New
World" after a two-year visit concluded, "I could not find any
other than that of *beautiful human beings.*"[27] The French,
more restrained since their exuberance over the Mirage and
always rather proprietary and patronizing toward the republic
they felt they hatched, nevertheless produced along with
mordant critics numbers of enthusiasts for the American
model. During the Orleanist monarchy and in the revolutionary risings of 1848, especially those of France and Germany,
champions of American principles made their influence felt
in the new constitutions proposed.

Between April and September of 1848 seven different
editions of the Constitution of the United States appeared in
France. The United States was the first to recognize the
Second Republic and the French overflowed with admiration.
Silvestre de Sacy, an Orleanist, called the American Union
one of the most admirable spectacles the earth had seen and a
model that Europe had been unable to equal. The foremost
writers of the republican papers affirmed and reaffirmed their
admiration. Strong countercurrents of official and unofficial
hostility to the United States set in during the 1850s, but
liberal and republican opponents of Napoleon III did not let
the legend or Mirage of American freedom die. They used
praise of American institutions as indirect criticism of the lack
of freedom in their own country.[28] Before and after the ill-
fated Frankfurt Assembly, German poets, political philoso-

---

[26] Ole Munch Raeder, *America in the Forties* (Minneapolis, 1929), 89.

[27] Fredrika Bremer, *The Homes of the New World: Impressions of America*, tr.
Mary Howitt (2 vols., New York, 1853), II, 144–45.

[28] Simon Jacob Copans, "French Opinion of American Democracy, 1852–1860"
(Ph.D. dissertation, Brown University, May 1942).

phers, and novelists sang praises of the transatlantic republic.[29]

Enthusiasts for America had been largely confined to Western Europe in the eighteenth century, but in the nineteenth they spread to Eastern Europe as well. Nationalist revolutionaries from Italy, Austria, Poland, and Hungary turned to America for guidance, inspiration, and aid. Alexander Farkas returned to Hungary from a visit to the United States coinciding with that of Tocqueville with "feelings of wonder, joy, hopes, and a thousand and one dreams" of his "beautiful new experience," and with "boundless respect."[30] A modern Polish writer declares that, "For decades the concept of America embraced all those things missing at home," including bread, land, freedom, and hope. "For a long time it [Poland has] needed America as a nascent utopia which was proof of what man could achieve when he was free."[31] Russian radicals and revolutionaries from the Decembrists of 1825, who believed "there were no good governments but in America," on through Alexander Herzen, Michael Bakunin, and Nicholas Chernyshevski looked to America as a beacon of hope, a promised land of progress.[32]

This reservoir of radical good will and enthusiasm for America began to run low in the late years of the nineteenth century. Many clung to their old convictions for a long time, and millions of working people continued to vote them with their feet as emigrants. But gradually the European Left and the European Right exchanged sides on America, with the Left moving away from its traditional role as champion to that

[29] Paul C. Weber, *America in the Imaginative German Literature in the First Half of the Nineteenth Century* (New York, 1926).

[30] Alexander Bölöni Farkas, *Journey in North America*, tr. Theodore and Helen Benedek Schoenman (Philadelphia, 1977), 219.

[31] Jerzy Jedlicke, "Images of America," *Polish Perspectives* XVIII (Nov. 1975): 33–34.

[32] Max M. Laserson, *The American Impact on Russia—Diplomatic and Ideological—1784–1917* (New York, 1950), 120–37, 244, and *passim*; David Hecht, *Russian Radicals Look to America, 1825–1894* (Cambridge, Mass., 1947), *passim*.

of critic and the Right moving in the opposite direction from longtime critic and detractor to a new role of defender and admirer.

In shedding their traditional attitudes toward the American Democracy, European conservatives took their lead to some extent from their brothers in Britain. The Anglo-American rapprochement toward the end of the century was conservatively inspired. British apostrophes to "our American Cousins" and to the "Anglo-Saxon Brotherhood" assumed anchorage in a common tradition of stability. The historian Edward A. Freeman discovered in 1883 that America was "still essentially an English land," its people in fact "more English" in many ways "than the kinsfolk they left behind in their older home," and the two were "in the higher sense one people."[33] And in the following reign, Frederic Harrison declared the American citizen "at heart much the same as the subject of King Edward."[34] Democratic, to be sure, but conservatively so. Equal, yes, but equality that reconciled antagonistic classes and fostered contentment. In seeing themselves and their like in the States, conservatives borrowed from James Bryce's *American Commonwealth* as they had once borrowed from Tocqueville for different purposes. While the amicable Scot had more complex things to say, he did lend support to the transformation of the American image: "The Americans are at bottom a conservative people," Bryce wrote, "in virtue both of the deep instincts of their race and of that practical shrewdness which recognises the value of permanence and solidarity in institutions. They are conservative in their fundamental beliefs, in the structure of government, in their social and domestic usages."[35] No subversive influences to fear from such a country.

Right-thinking people of this American sort deserved the

[33] Edward A. Freeman, *Some Impressions of the United States* (London, 1883), 16, 289; also W. E. Adams, *Our American Cousins* (London, 1883), 356.
[34] Frederic Harrison, *Memories and Thoughts* (New York, 1906), 174.
[35] James Bryce, *The American Commonwealth* (2 vols., London, 1888), II, 254.

admiration and support of conservative forces everywhere. They might in the future make useful allies as well. All countries of the West felt the explosive energy and expanding power of American industrial might. Its productivity and competitive impact became legendary. America's ventures in imperialism and her seizure of an overseas empire attracted other admirers. Rudyard Kipling, who was later to urge them to "take up the white man's burden," wrote, "Let there be no misunderstanding about the matter. I love this People, and if any contemptuous criticism has to be done, I will do it myself. My heart has gone out to them beyond all other peoples." Admitting their "massive vulgarity," he pronounced them "the biggest, finest, and best people on the surface of the globe!"[36] Kipling's contemporary, W. T. Stead, wrote a book entitled *The Americanization of the World* with the implicit thesis that such a transformation would be a jolly good thing. He was pleased to recount that two ducal families of Britain each had two American duchesses in succession and four statesmen of cabinet rank had American wives.[37] Conservatives elsewhere found that they could praise American achievements without admiring democracy. Hugo Münsterberg, the German psychologist who settled at Harvard, deplored the "popular notion" that "every American success must be to the glory of democracy," when in fact he believed its triumphs had come "in spite of" democracy.[38] On that assumption tributes from the conservative side came more easily.

From the radical side, in the meantime, tributes came ever harder. The very triumphs of America that conservatives celebrated were sources of disillusionment for the Left. Industrial growth brought trusts and monopolies and with them crises and unemployment, poverty and class conflict, inequal-

---

[36] Rudyard Kipling, *American Notes* (New York, n.d.), 192.
[37] W. T. Stead, *The Americanization of the World* (New York, 1901), 326.
[38] Hugo Münsterberg, *American Traits* (Boston, 1901), 189, 191.

ity and oppression just as in Europe. The Left expected these developments to come at greater speed and wider scale. America now produced villains for the Left—robber barons and monopolists; and also martyrs, those of Haymarket, Homestead, and Pullman. Democracy without social revolution was pronounced a delusion, and American society was held up as proof by the socialist parties that sprang up in nearly all European countries in the 1880s. Their Marxist leaders now joined in attacking the old transatlantic "workers' paradise" as the workers' purgatory, their hell upon earth, worse than anything in Europe. They tirelessly warned defecting proletarian emigrants against the lure of "bourgeois reform," of Americanism as a substitute for socialism. American freedom, they said, was freedom to exploit workers with unparalleled cruelty and brutality, and for workers themselves the freedom to submit to ruthless exploitation or starve. This new version of the old dream soon achieved a degree of orthodoxy. At the birth of the British Labour Party, its leaders denounced the American experience at least as bitterly as they condemned the state of things at home. That was to become an enduring tradition.[39]

Hard upon the leftist attack on the old myth of the workers' paradise, however, came the birth of a new and ironically turned invention of the Left, an American Promised Land for socialists. This followed logically from Marxist dialectic as then interpreted, which held that by necessity the expansion of capitalism called forth its antithesis, socialism. Since American capitalism was the most highly developed in the world, its trusts and monopolies the largest and most ruthless, their exploitation the cruelest, they would inevitably intensify the class struggle and be the first to drive the proletariat to their revolutionary task. They would precipitate crises sooner, and their very size and efficiency would smooth the way for socialist expropriation. The worse the evils of Ameri-

[39] Pelling, *America and the British Left*, 88.

can capitalism became, the better the prospects of American socialism. Friedrich Engels, Karl Marx's collaborator and supporter, repeatedly predicted an early advent of socialism in America and held that once the movement started it would go "with an energy and impetuousness compared with which we in Europe shall be mere children."[40]

The imminence and inevitable priority of socialism in the American Promised Land became part of the conventional wisdom among Marxists of Europe, who were often more European than scientific in their belief in American energy, efficiency, and impetuosity. The credo received unstinted endorsements from leaders of German socialism, the oldest and largest European party, from Karl Kautsky, from August Bebel, and from Wilhelm Liebknecht. French and English Marxists agreed that the hour of socialist fulfillment was at hand in America, and their prophesies went unchallenged as year after year they went unfulfilled. "We are waiting for you Americans to do something," Bebel told an American comrade in 1907. "You see, your country is far ahead of Germany in industrial development, and besides, you have compulsory education and a progressive republic—things for which we Germans are fighting."[41] The rhetoric about the new American Promised Land of socialism sometimes echoed that of the old, and for a time the legend seemed to have as secure a place in socialist folklore as its predecessor had enjoyed in earlier times. Even Lenin reflected it after the Russian Revolution in 1905. After the October Revolution of 1917, however, little more was heard about the American Promised Land for socialism. The ambivalence that mingled hope with hate disappeared on the Marxist Left as America was assigned the role of capitalist enemy of socialism everywhere.[42]

[40] R. Laurence Moore, *European Socialists and the American Promised Land* (New York, 1970), 12, 53–68.
[41] Ibid., 69–81, 100–102.
[42] Ibid., 103–33.

While the Left chose America as symbol of the capitalist enemy, the European intellectual elite of virtually *all* political persuasions from Left to Right increasingly fixed upon the same symbol to stand for worlds with which they found themselves at odds, either the world of the future already menacing the present, or a world of the past blocking a revolutionary future. The symbolism began before the First World War and grew thereafter. Sigmund Freud reflected it in telling his biographer Ernest Jones (in words recalling those of Buffon and Raynal) that "America is a mistake; a gigantic mistake, it is true, but none the less a mistake."[43] The attitude never wholly disappeared from Freud's mind.

Peter Gay has traced Freud's anti-American sentiments from their first expression in 1902, long before he set foot on these shores, and found that they ran through his whole life "like an unpleasant, monotonous theme." Many of these sentiments merely repeated the cultural arrogance and conde-scension common among European pronouncements on America for a century. "As a conventional, faultless, Euro-pean bourgeois, he thought about America as others thought," writes Gay. But he goes further to say that "slashing away at Americans wholesale; quite indiscriminately, with imaginative ferocity, Freud was ventilating some inner need," and that his anti-Americanism was not essentially about America at all. At times he appeared to have some inkling that his obsessive views were not entirely objective. He neverthe-less continued to vent his spleen in many ways, most embar-rassingly in collaborating with William Bullitt in a "psycho-logical study" of Woodrow Wilson by contributing what proved to be a caricature of applied analysis. He also stooped to hang a clinical classification on the victims of his bias. "To put it in technical terms," writes Gay, "he saw Americans one and all as victims of an anal-sadistic retentiveness, hostile to

[43] Ernest Jones, *The Life and Work of Sigmund Freud* (3 vols., New York, 1955), II, 59–60.

pleasure but conducive at the same time to the most aggressive conduct in business and politics."[44] So there.

Rainer Marie Rilke reflected some of these attitudes in 1913 when he wrote, "I no longer love Paris, partly because it is disfiguring and Americanizing itself." And later on so also did the writings of Bertolt Brecht, Louis-Ferdinand Céline, and Jean-Paul Sartre, among others. In their hands America had become a metaphor itself, an ambiguous and complex metaphor for what had gone wrong in Europe.[45] The latest example of this tradition, which still persists, is a book bearing the title *America* and published in English translation in 1988. It is the work of one Jean Baudrillard, a French sociologist from Nanterre to whom his publisher attributes "enormous recent influence." He marvels at "how little Americans have changed in the last two centuries," and wonders "what is there to criticize which has not been criticized a thousand times before." He manages, however, to find a number of items neglected by his predecessors. Baudrillard undertakes with great patience to help Americans understand "when they ask with such seriousness why other peoples detest them," find their culture so banal, so abominable, so utterly revolting. Confronted by the magnitude of the problem, he all but despairs of his efforts. "History and Marxism," he reflects, "are like fine wines and *haute cuisine*: they do not really cross the ocean."[46]

Modern European intellectuals borrowed selectively but copiously from earlier schools of criticism. From the early nineteenth-century aristocratic indictment of American culture they took the charge of materialism, of obsessive work, of the monetary measure of all things, the charge of uniformity, conformity, and dullness, of mediocrity and lack of distinction, of anti-intellectualism and cultural vulgarity, of sterility

[44] Peter Gay, *Freud. A Life for Our Time* (New York, 1989), 559–68.
[45] Richard Ruland, *America in Modern European Literature: From Image to Metaphor* (New York, 1976), 78, *et passim*.
[46] Jean Baudrillard, *America* (New York and London, 1988), 29–30, 79, 90, 91.

in the arts, letters, and sciences, and of repressive curbs on freedom. The moderns were more temperate than the early Tories had been in their strictures on democracy, but were inclined to agree with Bertrand Russell that American democracy had been degraded to the doctrine that "the majority know best about everything." On the doctrine of equality they agreed with Aldous Huxley that "nowhere has this system of humbug been brought to such perfection as in America."

The modern European intellectual elite borrowed also from the nineteenth-century radicals the concept of America as the Land of the Future, and from the conservative revisionists of the late nineteenth and early twentieth century they helped themselves to the vision of an Americanization of the world. The important difference was that these prophetic visions borrowed from the past were now seen as the fulfillment not of hopes but of fears. The future was to be dreaded and the Land of the Future was not a Promised Land but a "Menace," a "Cancer," an anti-utopia, the upside-down utopia of Huxley's *Brave New World*.[47]

By their use of the term "Americanization" Europeans were doing several things simultaneously. For one, they were assigning a geographical locality to a universal phenomenon. For another, they were making an assertion about moral responsibility, the allocation of blame. They were at once disclaiming culpability and giving it a national habitation and a name. The phenomena they included under the term "Americanization" were the less agreeable aspects of technological society and mass culture—in Europe as elsewhere. These included the fragmentation and depersonalization of life, the alienation of man from his work and from his fellow man, the abstractness, the standardization, and the mechanization of living, the erosion of moral values, and the subversion of traditional culture.

Surely none of these phenomena was peculiar to any one

[47] Aldous Huxley, *Brave New World* (London, 1932).

country. Rather they were characteristic of modernity in any nation. Yet America became the metaphor for them all. In assigning her that metaphorical role, Europeans were constructing a kind of alibi for themselves, a claim that the evils of which they complained were imposed on them from outside. Even the elite who abhorred the transformation admitted that it was far advanced in Europe and that, to quote Georges Duhamel, "For a handful of men who view the phenomenon with distrust and sadness, there are thousands who hail it with shouts." Mass defection within Europe made "Americanization" all the more ominous and insidious. "The American spirit," lamented Duhamel, "colonizes little by little such a province, such a city, such a house, such a soul."[48]

One of the earliest and perhaps the first to see through this particular self-serving image that Europeans possessed of Americans was Henry James. Many of the Americans that he shuttled back and forth across the Atlantic in his novels regularly discovered in Europe what they fled in America. Had Americans read their own writers with more attention they would have found that many of the traditional European strictures on American life and society had been anticipated at home. It was an authentic native American literary tradition of long standing, going all the way back to the old Federalists. For assaults on the farce of American democratic and egalitarian pretensions James Fenimore Cooper could hold his own with most European competitors. Poe once pronounced his country "the most odious and insupportable despotism that ever was heard of upon the face of the earth." And Melville could foresee the possibility of America as "An Anglo-Saxon China . . . In the Dark Ages of Democracy." The more repellent features of American life and history—the brutalities of slavery and its aftermath, the injustices of class and race, the

---

[48] Georges Duhamel, *America: The Menace* (Boston, 1931). The author preferred the original title, *Scènes de la vie future* (1931). W. T. Colyer, *America: A World Menace* (London, 1922) is a communist interpretation, as is also Robert Aron and Armand Dandieu, *Le Cancer americaine* (Paris, 1931).

corruptions of public and private life—have had their most uncompromising exposures and indictments from native, not from foreign writers. The level of American self-criticism reached in the pages of such writers as H. L. Mencken, Henry Miller, Theodore Dreiser, John Steinbeck, or William Faulkner has rarely been equaled in vehemence by European writings on America. As Marcus Cunliffe has observed, "There is no anti-Americanism so eloquent as that of the native American."[49] European writers have, in fact, often taken their cue and borrowed their models from American critics and reflected the pictures native writers have painted of their own country. Cue givers and takers reversed roles when the more guilt-ridden and self-hating anti-American Americans first imitated then outstripped their foreign models and became one of the richest inspirations of the European variety.

Americans should bring to bear another perspective on the history of European criticism, or what they often feel to be Europe's anti-Americanism. That perspective is the anti-Europeanism that Americans have perpetuated over the centuries. The United States from the beginning virtually defined itself morally in terms of anti-Europeanism: the Land of the Future versus a Europe of the bankrupt past. In sheer vituperation, few anti-Americans of any time or country could hold their own with the anti-Europeans of America in their prime. The works of Thomas Jefferson provide ample illustration. Jefferson once labeled four European monarchs fools, five of them idiots, and one, the King of Prussia, "a mere hog in body as well as in mind"—all produced by inbreeding, sensuality, luxury, and indolence. "And so endeth the book of Kings," he

[49] Marcus Cunliffe, "European Images of America," in Arthur M. Schlesinger, Jr. and Morton White, eds., *Paths of American Thought* (Boston, 1963), 511. A forthcoming book by Paul Hollander, *Anti-Americanism: Critiques at Home and Abroad, 1965–1990* (New York, 1991), stresses home talent over foreign in this field. Less than one-tenth of his 500 pages is devoted to Western Europe, most of the rest to American Anti-Americanism.

concluded. Nativism and xenophobia have been major and enduring issues of American politics, and the main targets of anti-foreign propaganda have been Europeans. On the other hand, in no European country was a national political party founded to promote anti-Americanism, such as the American, or Know-Nothing, Party, which was dedicated to the advancement of anti-Europeanism in America. Accompanying all this were towering pretensions of American moral superiority over other nations. America, so patriots declared over and over, was a country of innocence, virtue, happiness, and liberty, as against a Europe of vice, ignorance, misery, and tyranny. It is little wonder that Europeans have reacted rather sharply at times.[50]

The great creative period of European myth-making and metaphor-building about America came to a close before the Second World War. But anti-Americanism showed few signs of disappearing in postwar Europe. In his exhaustive study of anti-Americanism at home and abroad during the last quarter-century—years largely neglected in the present work—Paul Hollander finds the sentiment strongly rooted in Western Europe, though unevenly distributed. For one thing it is more prevalent in Protestant countries than in the Catholic nations of Italy and France. For another it is appreciably less apparent among the young than among their elders. Among intellectuals, East European countries for the present excepted, it is most widespread and achieves its most scornful and most impassioned forms. In intellectual circles it appears to be a blend of several elements, including a contempt for American culture, envy of American power, and apprehensions about American military and foreign policy. "Cultural imperialism" as manifest in the popularity of American mass culture— music, manners, morals, dress, entertainment—among European youth and common folk is a frequent complaint. Until very recently the rhetoric of anti-Americanism among mod-

[50]Cushing Strout, *The America Image of the Old World* (New York, 1963), 18–38.

ern intellectuals, at home as well as abroad, could equal or outdo any manifestation of earlier times for vehemence and ferocity.[51]

The old images and fantasies of the past—sometimes the remote past—still play a lingering part in present-day perceptions. For more than three centuries those American symbols and images formed a vivid theme in the Western mind. No history of the European imagination would be complete without it. No other modern country has bred for Europe quite so many fantasies. G. K. Chesterton once described an earlier version of Europe's America as "a fairyland of happy lunatics and loveable monsters."[52] Other versions have used less kindly language. We will recall that America has been described as a stupendous mistake as well as a fabulous utopia, and has served as a whipping boy for reactionaries and a model as well as an enemy for revolutionaries.

To the extent that America has ceased to be an imaginary land and become a real country, the European imagination is no doubt the poorer. It has been impoverished of many things—of mirages and nightmares, of promises and menaces, of yearnings and forebodings—not to mention assorted utopias and catastrophes. And along with these losses Europe has been—or should be by now—deprived of a metaphor that has served as an alibi for things that went wrong in Europe. But European losses should result in American gains. Living up to the demands of Europe's imaginary America has always put a strain on the nation's moral resources. It also helps account for the proliferation and durability of national myths and the energy that has gone into sustaining them. If America could accommodate herself to being somewhat less of a dream (or nightmare) and more of a reality—then the strain on the nation's moral resources would be lightened, and so would the burden of myth. And finally Europe's America might come nearer to resembling America herself.

[51] Hollander, *Anti-Americanism*, chap. 8.
[52] G. K. Chesterton, *What I Saw in America* (London, 1922), 265–66.

3

The Pursuit of Happiness

From the early years of the Republic, Americans have lived with an international reputation for excessive love of money and the obsessive pursuit of gain. They became accustomed to it. It came from all sides, friend and foe, and appeared to amount to an international consensus. It was expressed in varying degrees of opprobrium and was mixed at times with traces of envy or admiration. It continued in currency, decade after decade from the eighteenth century to the present. The word "materialism" apparently did not come into usage in this sense until the middle of the nineteenth century. It was soon marshalled for this purpose, though "American materialism" did not reach full notoriety until the twentieth century.

Long before the term "materialism" was applied to it, the idea had accumulated a considerable literature of elaboration. Reporting that a conversation between Americans was never heard without the word "dollar" being used, Mrs. Trollope remarked, "Such unity of purpose, such sympathy of feeling, can, I believe, be found nowhere else except, perhaps, in an ants' nest."[1] To Charles Dickens it appeared that "all their

[1] Frances Trollope, *Domestic Manners of the Americans*, ed. Donald Smalley (New York, 1949; original ed., 1832), 301.

40

cares, hopes, joys, affections, virtues, and associations seemed to be melted down into dollars."[2] Everything spiritual and temporal was measured in money. "And how they talk of money!" echoed a critic from the next century. "In snatches of conversation caught in the streets, the restaurants, and the cars . . . always 'dollars-dollars-dollars!'"[3]

These foreign characterizations of American life took on a less unflattering form when phrased as descriptions of American work habits. In that form they emphasized industriousness, energy, efficiency, and zeal for the task at hand. As Michel Chevalier put it, "The American mechanic is a better workman, he loves his work more, than the European. He is *initiated* not merely in the hardships, but also in the rewards, of industry."[4] A Scottish worker with three years in the States put it rather less attractively: "'Hurry up' is a phrase in the mouth of every person. . . . Work, work, work, is the everlasting routine of every day life. . . . To say that these people are extremely industrious would by no means convey a correct idea of their habits; the fact is they are selfish and savagely wild in devouring their work."[5] Adjustment to the pace of the American work-work-work ethic was a shock for European immigrant workers. They were warned by a Scottish businessman that they should not make the effort unless prepared "to do much more than even hard-working men do here,"[6] an adjustment that Anthony Trollope thought "to an English workman would be intolerable."[7] Sir Charles Lyell at mid-nineteenth century described "a country where all, whether rich or poor, were laboring from morning till night"

[2] Charles Dickens, *Martin Chuzzlewit* (New York, 1843–44), 273.

[3] Philip Burne-Jones, Bart., *Dollars and Democracy* (New York, 1904), 74.

[4] Michel Chevalier, *Society, Manners and Politics in the United States* (Boston, 1839), 430–31.

[5] James Dawson Burn, *Three Years Among the Working-Classes* (London, 1865), 11.

[6] John Leng, *America in 1876: Pencillings during a Tour in the Centennial Year: With a Chapter on the Aspects of American Life* (Dundee, 1877), 67.

[7] Anthony Trollope, *North America* (2 vols., London, 1862), I, 186.

and where "the national motto should be, 'All work and no play.'"[8] This foreign perception of American habits persisted in the next century. "The American not only works faster," wrote George Smart in 1912, "he walks faster,—everything he does is done more fiercely. He is increasing his pace continually. . . ."[9] And a German visitor of 1928 thought "This sense of hurry has permeated American homes; the women and even the children are imbued with it. Americans do not know what leisure is. . . ."[10]

In making such generalizations about work and leisure in America, those who mentioned the South at all in this connection did so to make an exception of it. The southerner was understood to "possess less of the enterprising spirit," to be fond "above all, of idleness," to give way to "indolence," and to cultivate leisure in a European and most un-American way.[11] The West, on the other hand, was quite a different story. "For the West is the most American part of America," as James Bryce saw it; "that is to say, the part where those features which distinguish America from Europe come out in the strongest relief. What Europe is to Asia, what England is to the rest of Europe, what America is to England, that the Western States and Territories are to the Atlantic States. . . . All is bustle, motion, and struggle. . . . They throw themselves into work with a feverish yet sustained intensity. They rise early, they work all day, they have few pleasures, few opportunities for relaxation. I remember in the young city of Seattle on Puget Sound [in the 1870s] to have found business in full

[8] Charles Lyell, A Second Visit to the United States of North America (2 vols., London, 1850), II, 91.

[9] George Thomas Smart, The Temper of the American People (Boston, 1912), 137.

[10] Arthur Feiler, America Seen Through German Eyes (New York, 1928), 259.

[11] Francis J. Grund, The Americans in Their Moral, Social, and Political Relations (Boston, 1837), 374; Alexis de Tocqueville, Democracy in America (New York, 1972), I, 395; II, 235; Chevalier, Society, Manners and Politics, 114–15; Thomas Holley Grattan, Civilized America (2 vols., London, 1859), II, 246; C. Vann Woodward, American Counterpoint: The North-South Dialogue on Slavery and Racism (Boston, 1971), 13–46.

swing at seven o'clock A.M.: the shops open, the streets full of people."[12]

Even in the streets of the effete East, Europeans were struck with the feverish bustle and connected it with what one called a "greater uniformity of stature, shape, feature, and expression, among both the men and women of America, than there is in England."[13] In spite of mixed origins, Anthony Trollope thought "no man has a type of face so clearly national as an American," who was "as completely marked as . . . any race under the sun." He attributed the uniformity to "hot-air pipes and . . . dollar-worship."[14] Captain Marryat was struck by "a remarkable family likeness among the people," so much so that every man on the street seemed to be "a brother or a connection of the last man who had passed me." He decided it was because "they were all intent and engrossed with the same object"—money, and that "this produced a similar contraction of the brow, knitting of the eyebrows, and compression of the lips—a similarity of feeling had produced a similarity of expression, from the same muscles being called into action."[15] Herbert Spencer lent his support to the theory. "I perceive in American faces generally," he said in 1882, "a great amount of determination—a kind of 'do or die' expression," which he associated with "a power of work exceeding that of any people."[16]

Europeans felt impelled to explain the national peculiarity they observed and offered numerous theories to account for the feverish striving of Americans and its concentration on pursuit of wealth. An obvious explanation was that there was so much wealth to be pursued, so many fortunes still to be

[12] James Bryce, *American Commonwealth* (2 vols., London, 1888), II, 681.

[13] James Silk Buckingham, *The Slave States of America* (2 vols., London, 1842), I, 487–88.

[14] A. Trollope, *North America*, I, 291.

[15] Frederick Marryat, *A Diary in America*, ed. Sydney Jackman (New York, 1962; original ed., 1839), 423–24.

[16] E. L. Youmans, *Herbert Spencer on the Americans and the Americans on Herbert Spencer* (New York, 1883), 11–12.

made, whereas in the Old World "the lottery is long since over . . . the great prizes are already drawn."[17] Another was the preoccupying challenge of an unbroken continent to be settled and subdued. Neither tradition nor law tied them to home or land. The Polish writer Adam G. Gurowski noticed that an American youth would announce a trip to Canton as casually as a European would plan a visit to a neighboring province. "Mobility urges the American incessantly to work, to undertake, to spread, create, produce," said Gurowski.[18]

A standard explanation for concentration on money-making was the relative absence of competing goals and interests. While Europeans of ambition and talent might pursue careers in literature, science, or the arts, Americans, in Tocqueville's damning opinion, were "swayed by no impulse but the pursuit of wealth."[19] He and many later critics assumed that politics in America were too petty and mean to attract ability of the first order. The pursuit of wealth had a peculiar attraction in a democracy. Since democracy ruled out distinction by title, rank, or heredity, wealth was likely to be the chief or only means of gaining status and distinction in society. Since the rules supposedly opened competition to all and since, as Achille Murat said, "every thing is to be won by competition: fortune, power, love," the stimulus to ambition was enormous, and the means of satisfying it was money.[20] One critic reflected the opinion of many in concluding that in America the "word money seems to stand as the representative of the word 'happiness' of other countries."[21] So the pursuit of happiness came to mean for many the pursuit of money.

Realizing that to indict a whole nation for cupidity was a

[17] Alexander Mackay, The Western World (2 vols., Philadelphia, 1849), II, 296; James Fullerton Muirhead, America the Land of Contrasts (London, 1898), 102–3.
[18] Adam G. Gurowski, America and Europe (New York, 1857), 151.
[19] Tocqueville, Democracy in America, II, 35.
[20] Achille Murat, A Moral and Political Sketch of the United States of America (London, 1833), 343.
[21] G. N. Featherstonehough, Excursions Through the Slave States (London, 1844), I, 281.

serious thing, foreign critics have at times tempered the indictment with various modifications. Few have denied that love of money was peculiarly strong in Americans, for that charge in one form or another has stuck with them for two centuries. What the more temperate or friendly commentators did was to advance another theory of American exceptionalism. Money and the getting of it had a different significance in America. Rather than the result of greed or avarice or rapacity, money was the "counter in the game," the only token or symbol of strivings that in Europe could find outlet in social, aesthetic, intellectual, or political achievements. The pursuit of money, said Gurowski, "becomes an intellectual drilling, and a test of skill. It becomes a game, deeply combined, complicated—a struggle with men and events, exciting, captivating, terrible. . . ."[22] As Hugo Münsterberg understood it, "Money is not the thing which is considered, but the manner of getting it."[23]

Behind the American's attitudes toward money were his deeper attitudes toward work, which George Smart thought he made a sort of religion: "he makes labor *per se* an obscuring idolatry. His joy of living is a joy of working, that exceeds the patient laboriousness of Europe; and the *élan* that Europe keeps for military and social life he keeps for work alone." Compared with the European, "The American works longer, to a later age, he has hardly yet begun to feel the monotony of labor or business."[24] Europeans deemed the work ethic a national trait, but considered its cult aspects the contribution of the business class. "The rough, broad difference between the American and the European business man," wrote Arnold Bennett, "is that the latter is anxious to leave his work, while the former is anxious to get to it. . . . It is not his toil, but his hobby, passion, vice, monomania."[25] As G. K. Chesterton

---

[22] Gurowski, *America and Europe*, 73–74.

[23] Hugo Münsterberg, *The Americans* (New York, 1904), 132, 235–36.

[24] Smart, *The Temper of the American People*, 81.

[25] Arnold Bennett, *Your United States* (New York and London, 1912), 93–94.

put it, "the American talks about his work and the Englishman about his holidays. His ideal is not labour but leisure."[26] The Americans, southerners excepted, either abominated leisure or did not know what to do with it; nor, it was generally agreed, did they really know what to do with the money they made.

For all that, European critics through the early years of the twentieth century were inclined to view American money-making as a youthful exuberance in response to unprecedented opportunity, a temporary obsession they would outgrow. Some went so far as to concede that "The American esteems money as money less than the Englishman of equal station,—less than the French *rentier*."[27] And a German believed that "in Europe materialism is more materialistic, brutality more brutal, and the dullness of life is even duller than in America, where spaciousness and plenty seem to soften and mellow these traits."[28] All along, however, the spaciousness was contracting, the opportunities were diminishing, and the scramble for riches was limited to fewer and fewer. Fortunes of the few became greater and the poverty of many more apparent. While Europe struggled out of the ruins of the First World War and watched the great boom of prosperity across the Atlantic, the rhetoric of criticism took on a sharper edge.

"Materialism" had been associated with Americanism in the European vocabulary for three-quarters of a century, but in 1926 America became "the Baphomet of the age—Materialism gross and unrefined, bloated with the wind of strange beliefs."[29] In the titles that books on the subject took in that period America was variously described as a *Midas*, in two titles as a *Menace*, in another a *Cancer*, in still another as a *Babbit Warren*, and in a French title simply as *The Enemy*. It

[26] G. K. Chesterton, *What I Saw in America* (London, 1922), 105.
[27] Smart, *The Temper of the American People*, 80.
[28] Feiler, *America Seen Through German Eyes*, 282.
[29] George Harmon Knoles, *The Jazz Age Revisited: British Criticism of American Civilization During the 1920's* (Stanford, London, 1955), 31.

was not only a menace to its own people, but to European civilization as well. It sold everything. It was a plutocracy untrammelled, without countervailing forces of civil service, army, or navy, much less aristocracy. Business ruled all it surveyed. Amateur anthropologists of the previous century had pointed out that Americans *pay* visits rather than *make* them, that they incur social *debts* and discharge them with interest, that "everything in America is a matter of business. A dinner is a transaction of barter, for which another equally good is expected. . . ."[30] The twentieth-century school of amateur anthropologists extended the old thesis to embrace the commercialization and business domination of an entire culture—church, state, school and press, marriage, family, home, and club, art, literature, all. It was a machine civilization, "a paradise for Robots." It was "organized to produce things rather than people, with output set up as a god." André Siegfried, the critic last quoted, added: "In its pursuit of wealth and power, America has abandoned the ideal of liberty to follow that of prosperity."[31] As pictured by extremists, it was a society without a soul. In its extreme form this indictment of the business civilization in America matches the severity of rhetoric leveled later on at the "blue ants" and their masters in modern collectivist societies.

The charge of materialism carried with it the charge of an indifference to the non-material in civilization, the life of the mind and imagination, the world of arts, letters, science, and learning. Long before the label of "materialism" gained currency, the new republic's shortcomings in this realm were the subject of consensus among European commentators. A famous early statement of their point of view by Sydney Smith in the *Edinburgh Review* of 1820 is worth recalling. Summing up the first forty years of independence of the Americans, he declared that "they have done absolutely nothing for the

---

[30] Gurowski, *America and Europe*, 377; Grattan, *Civilized America*, II, 93.
[31] André Siegfried, *America Comes of Age* (New York, 1927), 69, 348.

Sciences, for the Arts, for Literature, or even for statesman-like studies of Politics or Political-Economy." And then his battery of contemptuous questions, "In the four quarters of the globe, who reads an American book? or goes to an American play? or looks at an American picture or statue? What does the world yet owe to American physicians or surgeons . . . ? What new constellations have been discovered by the tele-scopes of Americans?"[32] The poverty of arts remained a persistent theme in the European commentary on American civilization for the next century. Few critics went so far as the French author in the 1850s whose chapter entitled *"Les Beaux-Arts en Amerique"* consisted of three perfectly blank pages.[33] But it was a standard theme among French writers such as Balzac, Stendhal, to some extent Hugo, and on through Renan and Taine.[34]

The main question among Europeans in the nineteenth century was not the extent of this cultural poverty but the reason for it and particularly whether the basic cause was democracy and equality. Tocqueville readily acknowledged that "in few of the civilized nations of our time have the higher sciences made less progress than in the United States; and in few have great artists, distinguished poets, or celebrated writers been more rare." He went on to say there were "no great historians and not a single eminent poet," and that Americans looked on literature "with a kind of disapprobation" and were "averse to general ideas. . . ." He was less clear, however, about the connection between these shortcomings and the existence of democracy. On the one hand he deplored the tendency of many Europeans to regard this "as a natural and inevitable result of equality," for that was "to mingle, uninten-tionally, what is democratic with what is only American." He pointed out that the situation of the Americans was "quite

[32] *The Edinburgh Review* XXXIII (Jan. 1820): 78–80.
[33] A. D'Alembert, *Flânerie parisienne aux Etats Unis* (Paris, 1856), 145–47.
[34] Simon Jacob Copans, "French Opinion of American Democracy, 1852–1860" (Ph.D. dissertation, Brown University, May 1942).

exceptional," and that there were "a thousand special causes," including "their exclusively commercial habits" that tended "to divert their minds from the pursuit of science, literature, and the arts . . . to fix the mind of the American upon the purely practical objects" and to draw him "earthward." On the other hand, he could sometimes support the opposite view, as when he wrote: "There is no class . . . in America in which the taste for intellectual pleasures is transmitted with hereditary posture and leisure and by which the labors of the intellect are held in honor. *Accordingly*, there is an equal want of the desire and the power of application to these objects." And again he wrote that "*the reason*" for the absence of great writers was that "freedom of opinion does not exist in America," a circumstance he attributed to the tyranny of the majority in a democracy.[35]

As was natural to expect, the more conservative critics generally fixed upon democracy and equality as the real reason for the American desert of the beaux arts. According to Captain Basil Hall, "one of the effects of democracy" was "unquestionably, to lower the standard of intellectual attainment, and, also, by diminishing the demand for refinement of all kinds, to lessen the supply." Under these circumstances "it would be the most unreasonable thing imaginable to expect the arts and sciences to flourish."[36] Thomas Hamilton agreed that the democratic society of America provided no leisure, no audience, no sympathy, and no encouragement for arts, letters, and learning, and that taste and enlightenment among "the younger portion of the richer classes" were markedly lower than that of their fathers' generation.[37] The artist in America, observed Thomas Colley Grattan, was "disappointed and dyspeptic" and those artists who could fled to

[35] Tocqueville, *Democracy in America*, I, 52, 265, 315; II, 35–37.

[36] Captain Basil Hall, *Travels in North America* (2 vols., Philadelphia, 1829), II, 55.

[37] Thomas Hamilton, *Men and Manners in America* (2 vols., Philadelphia, 1833), I, 194–96; also F. Trollope, *Domestic Manners of the Americans*, 330.

Europe. "In his own country he must be little better than a drudge, with incompetent critics and niggardly patrons, excluded from 'fashionable' society." "Democracy secures great physical enjoyment to a people," he wrote, "but it cramps the nation's intellect." It was America's fate "to do the labour of the world. All the higher duties of human improvement are done for her. The exercises of lofty thought, and the elegances of art, all come from Europe." In all this America was a consumer, not a producer.[38] "The lamp of artistic truth burns with a feeble flame; and mediocrity is allowed to take the highest place," wrote Sir Lepel Griffin in 1884; "in no department of art, has any work, drama, novel, poem, painting, or musical composition been produced which could justly be placed in the first class."[39]

Americans laughed at the posturing of Oscar Wilde, but they took Matthew Arnold with terrible seriousness, though he reached his conclusions before coming to America. There was little they could do about what Arnold called the "want of what is elevated and beautiful, of what is interesting" by which he explained the "great void" in American civilization. These deficiencies included "ancientness," and he specified cathedrals, parish churches, feudal castles, and Elizabethan country homes. He also found the landscape "not interesting" and the climate harsh. He assured Americans in the most "friendly" fashion, he said, that "the great bulk of the nation" were Philistines, "a livelier sort of Philistine than ours," but a greater percentage. He quoted Renan on "their intellectual mediocrity, their vulgarity of manners, their superficial spirit, their lack of general intelligence." Yet they were irretrievably given to self-flattery. Arnold was quite prepared to admit that democracy had solved "the human problem," the problems of economics and politics, but he held that "everything is against distinction," particularly "the glorification of the common

[38]Grattan, *Civilized America*, I, 235; II, 96, 106, 110–11.
[39]Griffin, *The Great Republic*, 97.

man." Washington and Hamilton were distinguished, but they "belong to the pre-American age"; Lincoln had many virtues, but "not distinction." Arnold entertained doubts that anything of true excellence and distinction was forthcoming from the democracy.[40]

Other Victorian greats added their bit to the picture in their individual styles. Carlyle hailed "the supreme achievement of the American people," which was "to have begotten, with a rapidity beyond recorded example, Eighteen Millions of the greatest bores ever seen in this world before." And Ruskin saluted their "lust of wealth, and trust in it; vulgar faith in magnitude and multitude, instead of nobleness; . . . perpetual self-contemplation issuing in passionate vanity; total ignorance of the finer and higher arts. . . ."[41]

Americans derived what soothing they could from the salve with which James Bryce usually applied his criticism. "All things considered," he wrote, "I doubt whether democracy tends to discourage originality, subtlety, refinement, in thought and expression." He pointed out that arts and literature had been debased and vulgarized "under absolute monarchies and under oligarchies." This was not to deny the deficiencies mentioned. In fact his appraisal was rather similar to Arnold's. "Life is not as interesting in America . . . as it is in Europe," he said flatly; "because society and the environment of men are too uniform." He too mentioned the absence of "objects which appeal to the imagination," including those "castles gray with age." It was not merely a question of why America "has given us few men of highest and rarest distinction, but whether it has failed to produce its fair share of talents of the second rank." Granted there was a distinctive note in American letters that "may be caught by ears not the most delicate," he professed his inability to say which "peculiarity

---

[40] Matthew Arnold, *Civilization in the United States* . . . (Freeport, N.Y., 1972), 127, 173, 176–89.
[41] Quoted in Pelling, *America and the British Left*, 3.

of American literature is due to democracy." No, the question remained, "why the trans-Atlantic branch, nowise inferior in mental force, contributes less than its share to the common stock," for they "draw from Europe far more than they send to her, while of art they produce little and export nothing." Bryce thought "the causes lie deeper." He mentioned tentatively the hustle and bustle, the exciting distractions, the lack of patience and time, and the lack of an atmosphere "charged with ideas as in Germany" or with "critical *finesse* as in France." He hoped cheerfully that time would change all that.[42]

Low estimates of American culture explained by the affects of democracy and equality were not confined to conservative Europeans, for they were often shared by radicals of the twentieth century. The English socialist Beatrice Webb believed that "there is something in the way of life and the mental environment of the U.S.A that hinders or damps down the emergence of intellectual or artistic distinction." She observed that America in the previous generation had produced "no men or women in any way comparable in mental force to a Bismarck, a Renan, or a Darwin," or for that matter "to the host of literary men" and men of genius turned out every year by "the three great European races." She explained this deficiency by "two radically false assumptions with which all Americans start their career. . . ." The second of these was their addiction to classical economic theory, but first and foremost "of these fallacies is the old constitutional maxim that 'all men are born free and equal' . . ." This doctrine prevented Americans from showing proper respect to intellectuals with "real originality of outlook or intensity of talent." In England, on the other hand, she said, "the old attitude of reverence to kings, nobles, priests has been gradually transferred to men of distinction during the transitional years from political oligarchy to political democracy." Mrs. Webb once described herself as "the cleverest member of one of the

42 Bryce, *American Commonwealth*, II, 437, 617–18, 622–28, 641.

cleverest families in the cleverest class of the cleverest nation of the world," claims that probably did not gain immediate endorsement in America. She observed during a visit to the country in 1898 that "the very qualities he [the American] most needs" were "reverence for authority and historical knowledge of human affairs."[43] The first extensive communist critique of civilization in the United States appeared in 1922 under the title *Americanism: A World Menace.* The author wrote contemptuously of the "intellectual and spiritual poverty of American life," scorned its pretensions of equality and democracy, and attributed the vulgarization of culture to the power of big business.[44]

Not all European critics were so harsh or sweeping in their estimates of American cultural strivings, and there were some who offered words of encouragement, though most often in a patronizing manner. Even an occasional Frenchman such as Paul Bourget could speak of the appearance of "admirable American artists" and discount "the prediction that there will never be any American art."[45] A German pundit could note with approval the appearance of museums, orchestras, and theaters, though adding that the source of these activities was "not the creative genius, but the average citizen, in his striving after self-perfection and culture."[46] From time to time Europeans were belatedly discovering or rediscovering a Winslow Homer or a George Innis or a John Singer Sargent, a St. Gaudens or a Remington, and perennially rediscovering jazz and attributing it to Africa. Brooklyn Bridge received due praise and later the George Washington Bridge. The Europeans had least trouble agreeing on admiration for twentieth-century architecture, though they did not always admire the same things or the right things. Mainly they

43 Beatrice Webb, *American Diary,* ed. David A. Shannon (Madison, 1963), 40, 146–47. Her self-characterization is quoted by the editor in his introduction, xii–xvi.
44 W. T. Colyer, *Americanism: A World Menace* (London, 1922), II, 33, 78–79.
45 Paul Bourget, *Outre-Mer: Impressions of America* (New York, 1895), 370.
46 Münsterberg, *The Americans,* 361.

were staggered by the skyscrapers and lavishly admired their vitality, even when adding that they were more the product of engineering than art, or were "for the most part entirely a matter of economics." Still, they were the perfect expression of American civilization and a relief from the "classic banalities" of Washington's Roman temples, or the "Gothic monstrosities" of public architecture. Few foreign critics appear to have noticed industrial or domestic architecture, and almost none appear to have heard of the architectural genius of the age, Louis H. Sullivan.[47] Along with detractors and deplorers, American arts won a few champions, mainly amateurs. Arnold Bennett was exasperated by the failure of upperclass Americans to appreciate native genius, especially in the theater and in industrial architecture.[48] Sir Philip Gibbs, a popular novelist, could be quite carried away by his enthusiasm for a predicted American Golden Age. It would be "fresh and springlike, and rich in vitality and promise," like the Elizabethan period because Americans were "hearty, healthy, and rich," much like the Elizabethans.[49]

In the meantime, pending the flowering of an Elizabethan Yankeedom, European skeptics carried on their venerable tradition of finding no oasis in the American cultural desert. "There is no culture in America," wrote G. Lowes Dickinson, philosopher and critic. He declared that, "Nowhere on that continent," was there any class who "respect not merely art but the artistic calling. Broadly, business is the only respectable pursuit."[50] In the twenties C. N. Bretherton echoed, "America has not, at present, any civilization of its own." Looking ahead he asked, "Will the Americans of a hundred years hence have any intellect?" The answer was,

[47] Knoles, *The Jazz Age Revisited*, 104–24; Andrew J. Torrielli, *Italian Opinion on America* (Cambridge, 1941), 238.

[48] Bennett, *Your United States*, 100–101, 137, 163–67.

[49] Philip Gibbs, *People of Destiny: Americans As I Saw Them at Home and Abroad* (New York, 1920), 156–57.

[50] G. Lowes Dickinson, *Appearances* (New York, 1914), 194, 198.

"they will, if they proceed along the road they are now taking, have none at all."[51] Hilaire Belloc thought an indigenous national literature had not even begun.[52] A German editor concluded that "Material prosperity covers up an inner void. Probably the American atmosphere is a handicap to cultural progress."[53] André Siegfried declared that "modern America has no national art and does not even feel the need of one." It sacrificed all to "material progress."[54] The classic speculation about what the future archaeologists would find in the ruins produced one Cassandra who doubted there would be anything at all to indicate a loss to mankind.[55] Another, Georges Duhamel, agreed that, "Should it fall into ruins tomorrow, we should seek in its ashes in vain for the bronze statuette that is enough to immortalize a little Greek village. Ruins of Chicago!—prodigious heap of iron-work, concrete, and old plaster."[56] And there were still more Cassandras. "Meanwhile, on the western side of the Atlantic," wrote Aldous Huxley, "the progressive falsification of values steadily continues."[57]

If our European critics have found the American cultural scene so desolate, what profit or reward could they have found in exploring it so often and at such length? What *justification* did they find for such efforts? They have spilled barrels of ink on the subject through the centuries. Speculating on their outpourings, Harold Laski, who contributed more than his share of the ink, once wrote: "In the complex relationship between the European tradition and Americanism, the European has found it hard to surrender his right to patronize the American. He has had, therefore, to find some way of ratio-

[51] C. H. Bretherton, *Midas: or the United States and the Future* (London, 1926), 64, 86.

[52] Hilaire Belloc, *The Contrast* (New York, 1924), 183.

[53] Feiler, *America Seen Through German Eyes*, 263.

[54] Siegfried, *America Comes of Age*, 350.

[55] Elijah Brown, *The Real America* (London, 1913), 3–5.

[56] Georges Duhamel, *America: The Menace* (New York, 1931), 86.

[57] Aldous Huxley, *Jesting Pilate* (London, 1926), 279.

nalizing this right."[58] I think the fundamental rationalization amounts to an unacknowledged consensus about American civilization among European critics. Vaguely formulated as it was, it could be shared by both friendly and unfriendly commentators with contrasting implications. It appeared in the eighteenth century and collected a variety of adherents in the next two hundred years.

In the final lines of the book on his American travels in 1788, Brissot de Warville gave the more friendly turn to the conception. First he pointed out that the way to despotism lay through men of power, ambition, and genius using the ignorant populace to destroy "the enlightened but aristocratic middle order." But then, he cheerfully added, "Here in America there are no men of great power, no men of genius, no aristocratic middle order, no populace." Lacking both men of genius and ignorant masses, America escaped despotism. "General prosperity can be found only in this mean," he wrote.[59] Brissot would probably not have been averse to calling "this mean" of his the Golden Mean, *le juste milieu*. Nor would La Rochefoucauld, who used the same concept in as friendly a way.[60] Less sympathetic critics, who also found the idea useful, have called it "the way of mediocrity." Instead of the Golden Mean, perhaps a Brazen Mean. Between the mean conceived as golden and that conceived as brazen stretched the flexible bounds of the European consensus on America.

Tocqueville, as usual, fell between the extremes, but well within the broad consensus. At the conclusion of his *Democracy in America*, he summed up the thesis that ran through many of his pages: the painful dilemma with which

[58] Harold Laski, *The American Democracy: A Commentary and an Interpretation* (New York, 1948), 724.

[59] Brissot de Warville, *New Travels in the United States* . . . , ed. Durand Echeverria (Cambridge, Mass., 1964), 424.

[60] François Alexander Frédéric, duc de La Rochefoucauld-Liancourt, *Travels Through the United States* . . . (2 vols., London, 1799), II, 678–79.

America confronted the modern world. There was no country in the world, he observed more than once, where "there are so few ignorant and at the same time so few learned individuals." One's estimate of America depended on "what is wanted of society, and its government." If the object were "to refine the habits, embellish the manners, and cultivate the arts, to promote the love of poetry, beauty, and glory," that was one thing. If on the other hand, the goals were "the production of comfort and the promotion of well-being," if it were "to ensure the greatest enjoyment and to avoid the most misery," that was another. He compared losses with gains. In the democratic world, "The sentiment of ambition is universal, but the scope of ambition is seldom vast. . . . life is not adorned with brilliant trophies, but it is extremely easy and tranquil. . . . genius becomes more rare, information more diffuse. . . . less perfection, but more abundance in all the productions of the arts. . . . Almost all extremes are softened or blunted: all that was most prominent is superseded by some middle term, at once less lofty and less low, less brilliant and less obscure, than what before existed in the world." Tocqueville confessed that "the sight of such universal uniformity chills and saddens me," but conceded that this feeling stemmed from his "own weakness." In the sight of the Creator, he believed that a "state of equality is perhaps less elevated, but it is more just: and its justice constitutes its greatness and beauty."[61]

Europeans since Tocqueville have played many variations on this theme. They have tried to capture their meaning in a variety of metaphors—some more flattering than others. "If the social structure . . . has no florid Corinthean capital rising into the clear air above," wrote Alexander Mackay, "neither has it a pedestal in the mire beneath." Wanting in ornament, it was "also wanting in much of the painful and

[61] Tocqueville, *Democracy in America*, I, 51–52, 252–53, 315; II, 247–48, 331–34.

degrading."[62] In Europe, as Anthony Trollope put it, men stood "on a long staircase, but the crowd congregates near the bottom," whereas "in America men stand upon a common platform, but the platform is raised above the ground, though it does not approach in height the top of our staircase."[63] Granting much "general well-being among the people at large," Thomas C. Grattan added: "Each man at all elevated in the social scale seems to pay a certain *per centum* of his better qualities—a sort of intellectual property-tax into the public treasury of morals," thus leaving no one outstanding. Minus what he called "the splendid contrasts of the European system," he thought that "a medium civilization is alone feasible." No towering peaks and no abyss: only the green and placid plains of American democracy.[64] Even so stalwart a pro-American as John Bright conceded that the advance of general intelligence came at the cost of individual eminence, but held that "instead of individual greatness you have the greatness of a nation."[65]

It was certainly the golden rather than the brazen side of the American mean that James Bryce held up in this passage: "Life in America is in most ways pleasanter, easier, simpler than in Europe; it floats in a sense of happiness like that of a radiant summer morning." Yet he followed that with the qualification that "life in any of the great European countries is capable of an intensity, a richness blended of many elements, which has not yet been reached in America."[66] This lacked the sting of Tocqueville's estimate: "Nothing conceivable is so petty, so insipid, so crowded with petty interests—in one word, so anti-poetic—as the life of a man in the United States."[67] Yet the latter was probably nearer to the center of

[62] Mackay, *The Western World*, II, 296.
[63] A. Trollope, *North America*, II, 315.
[64] Grattan, *Civilized America*, I, 81–82; II, 471.
[65] Quoted in Pelling, *America and the British Left*, 22.
[66] Bryce, *American Commonwealth*, II, 676.
[67] Tocqueville, *Democracy in America*, II, 74.

the European consensus than the former. If America, said G. Lowes Dickinson, "is not burdened by masses lying below the average, [she] is also not inspired by an elite rising above it. Her distinction is the absence of distinction. No wonder Walt Whitman sang the 'Divine Average.' There was nothing else in America for him to sing."[68] George Santayana put it more genially: "American life is a powerful solvent. It seems to neutralize every intellectual element, however tough and alien it may be, and to fuse it in the native good-will, complacency, thoughtlessness, and optimism."[69]

Most Europeans of the classes from which the critics of American life came were prepared to concede that it was good enough, even better than Europe, for working-class people— but not for them. "These people are happy," wrote Fanny Kemble, "—their wants are satisfied, their desires fulfilled— their capacities of enjoyment meet with full employment . . . but how is it with me?" That was another matter. "The heart of a philanthropist may indeed be satisfied, but the intellectual man feels a dearth that is inexpressibly painful."[70] Sir Charles Lyell, the famous geologist, who made four extended visits to America, thought that for the laboring class it was "the land where they are best off, morally, physically, and intellectually"; yet he declared he had "no wish whatever to live there" himself.[71] Lord Bryce said he had "never met a European of the upper or middle classes who did not express astonishment when told that America was a more agreeable place than Europe to live in. 'For working men,' he would answer, 'yes' . . ." Bryce was one of the few of his time— though many joined him later—who could find appeals in American life "which may well make a European of any class prefer to dwell there." Prominent among these appeals were

---

[68] Dickinson, *Appearances*, 141.

[69] George Santayana, *Character and Opinion in the United States* (New York, 1956).

[70] Frances A. Kemble, *Journal of a Residence in America* (Paris, 1835), 55n.

[71] Lyell, *A Second Visit to the United States*, II, 217.

those that sprang from the very source of traditional upper-class disdain—that is, equality. There was, he thought, "a certain charm, hard to convey,"—but more good nature, heartiness, frankness, ease "than is possible in countries where every one is either looking up or down." Whatever it was—and he thought equality was the key—it enabled people "to take their troubles more lightly than they do in Europe." But against that he admitted one "serious drawback—its uniformity"—that dreadful uniformity that had been and remained the common complaint. "Travel where you will," he observed, "you feel that what you have found in one place you will find in another."[72]

The question remained whether with all their equality and uniformity, their energy and their zeal, their bustle and abundance the Americans had enjoyed any genuine success in their pursuit of happiness. Another form the question took was whether the happiness they claimed to enjoy was worthy of the name. The arcadian bliss attributed to post-Revolutionary America for a period was largely a projection of European dreams. But then the doubts and denials they later developed were largely the projections of European fears and darker moods. The assessment of another people's happiness is necessarily a subjective exercise. Subjective or not, our critics often thought they perceived signs of unhappiness, strains of melancholy, emptiness, and inner loneliness running through American life. Although he thought these people were "placed in the happiest circumstances that the world affords," it seemed to Tocqueville that "a cloud habitually hung, upon their brow," that they were "serious and almost sad, even in their pleasures," and that they were haunted by "that strange melancholy" which he associated with democracy, "easy circumstances," and uniformity.[73] A century later a sympathetic German observer of Americans spoke of an

[72] Bryce, American Commonwealth, II, 660–74.
[73] Tocqueville, Democracy in America, II, 136–39.

"inner loneliness" and "a feeling of dissatisfaction which prevents them from being fundamentally at peace," a malaise they "try to cover up" by "hurrying and rushing" and feverish "outward activity."[74] A generally benign Englishman who eventually became an American citizen, thought there were "more lonely people in the United States than in any population of equal size in European lands." He arrived at a conclusion that we may hope he overcame before taking out naturalization papers. "For a country that makes 'the pursuit of happiness' one of its political programs," he wrote, "America has stupendously failed."[75] A contemporary and most unbenign compatriot of his searched "the hurrying, stampeding thousands," in American streets in vain for "one face that looks happy or contented, or even satisfied with his lot."[76]

A sunnier side of the national disposition had been noted by many other European critics—all the way back to Crevecœur, including Barbé-Marbois, Brissot, Chevalier, Grund, Gurowski, Bremer, Cobden, Bryce, Kipling, Muirhead. All that heartiness, cheerfulness, good-natured humility, outgoing hopefulness, all that optimistic fatalism or fatalistic optimism could not be wholly denied by the Cassandras. But even their concessions were linked with a denial. Thus Captain Marryat: "Again, I repeat, the Americans are the happiest people in the world in their own delusions."[77] Or that most consummate of Irish snobs, Thomas Colley Grattan: "They possess one great element of true happiness in a general placidity of temper, although it arises from a negative cause."[78] And finally, a rarer philosophic, if sardonic, spirit, Aldous Huxley in the role of Diogenes investigating American happiness in Los Angeles, the "City of Dreadful Joy," he called it. There was, indeed, joy in America. "And what joy!

[74] Feiler, *America Seen Through German Eyes*, 56–57, 260–61.
[75] Smart, *The Temper of the American People*, 110–11, 167.
[76] Brown, *The Real America*, 95.
[77] Marryat, *A Diary in America*, 162. Emphasis added.
[78] Grattan, *Civilized America*, II, 317.

The joy of rushing about, of always being busy, of having no time to think, of being too rich to doubt." It provoked even darker reflections: "In modern America the Rome of Cato and the Rome of Heliogabalus coexist and flourish with an unprecedented vitality." And all this among a people "unaware of war or pestilence or famine or revolution." It made him wonder if the "truest patriots" were not "those who pray for a national calamity."[79]

It has been noted before that for every trait attributed to the national character, its opposite has been attributed with equal conviction if not equal authority. One would not expect to find in Hilaire Belloc, the Catholic poet, novelist, historian, and indomitable champion of thirteenth-century values, the antithesis of the prophets of American doom. Yet it was Belloc who could write that "the Americans were happier than any people of the Old World," indeed "much happier," in fact "the happiest white people in the modern world." And he thought "the cause of the happiness is Candour," for "The American people live in truth," and with "that sort of freedom in the soul which is the breeding soil of happiness."[80]

Unimpeded and uninformed by these contradictory advices from abroad, the Americans continued, as they had from the time of their eighteenth-century proclamation of the policy, their pursuit of happiness—with success perhaps as widely varied as their numerous European critics' estimates of their happiness.

[79] Huxley, *Jesting Pilate*, 267–68, 287.
[80] Belloc, *The Contrast*, 72.

4

America
As Metaphor

How was it possible for Europeans to fit the emerging American nation into their traditional scheme of things and ways of thinking? It was an entirely new experience at the time to have major colonies break away in concerted action by revolution and form an independent nation. There were no precedents from their own history to shape their thinking. Was the new nation to be thought of as an extension of themselves, a transplanted copy, an offspring? Or was this handiwork of revolutionists something barbarously alien, something without precedent or roots?

As if to improvise an answer to such questions and reassure the Europeans—but mainly to please and flatter themselves—American revolutionists promptly began to memorialize their deeds and their nation as the new embodiment of Roman virtue, the fabled virtue of the Republic. They adopted Roman symbols, styles, and names, and emblazoned Latin quotations and mottoes on stone, coin, seal, and architecture. They lost no time about it. American colleges began to refer to their turf as the "campus" in 1774 (the first one at Princeton); the government acquired a "Senate" in 1775 and a "capitol" before one was built. The first political parties, with a Latin flourish, called themselves Federalists and Republicans. The great seal of the United States bore an eagle, suggesting that of Caesar's legions, plus an enigmatic Latin phrase on one side, and on the other side two more Latin phrases and the date 1776 in Roman, not Arabic, numerals. Breaking with British pounds and shillings, Jefferson chose the decimal system for coinage, and coins were minted with an eagle on one side and a goddess in classical garb (despite official disavowal of gods or goddesses) on the other. Eventually the *fasces*, emblem of his legal power borne before the Roman lictor, turned up on American coins and elsewhere. Despite the absence of Roman law, Roman ruins, roads, or temples, the Roman iconography continued to flourish in the New World's first republic. States also built "capitols" and regularly topped their domes with goddesses in classical garments. Twenty states used Latin mottoes on their great seals.[1]

European nationals, with a somewhat more legitimate Roman heritage, were not much taken with the American posturing—at least until the French began to imitate them during their own revolution. Other Europeans of a friendly disposition thought the new nation might do better by way of models and symbols. In a letter to the Reverend James Madison of the College of William and Mary in January, 1783, the Marquis de Chastellux came forth with an attractive alternative. Deploring the American fad of embracing Roman symbols and thinking of themselves as modern Roman republicans, the Marquis pronounced the model unworthy of them. The Romans, he wrote, were "ferocious, unjust, grasping by nature," in short barbarians. Moreover they were "ostentatious from vanity," and while "able to purchase masterpieces

---

[1] Howard Mumford Jones, *O Strange New World* (Cambridge, Mass., 1970), has a good chapter on "Roman Virtue" in the early republic.

of art," they had "not a taste for the arts" themselves. "The Americans," on the other hand, "proceeding in general from the most polished countries of Europe, have no barbarous prejudices to cast off. They ought rather to compare themselves to the Greek colonies; and certainly Syracuse, Marseilles, Crotona, and Agrigentum had no reason to envy their mother cities," any more than the Americans had to bow to "the pedantic enactments of Cambridge, Oxford, and Edinburgh."[2]

The Greek colony metaphor carried much appeal for Europeans while they were still in the transports of their American dream in the post-revolutionary period. Abbé Brizard gave added currency to the notion in his *Fragment de Xenophon*, based on the fiction of a newly recovered Greek manuscript describing an ancient Greek colony in America that outdid the motherland in a golden age of liberty, art, and prosperity. Others spoke of Franklin, Washington, Jefferson, Adams, and their contemporary American patriots as the modern counterparts of the philosopher guardians in Plato's *Republic*.[3] Jean Baptiste Say reflected the idea in a letter to Thomas Jefferson in 1803, in which he said, "The United States are the children of Europe," and went further to say that "the children are greater than the parents" and would liberate them from their ancient prejudices.[4]

The flattering metaphor of America as a Greek colony that started with a culture fully matured quickly faded with the passing of Europe's American mirage after the French Revolution. America suddenly began to seem different, alien, young in the sense of being raw, gauche, immature, if not alien. The duc de La Rochefoucauld-Liancourt put it gently

[2]Chastellux to the Rev. James Madison, January 12, 1783, in Chastellux, *Travels in North America, in the Years 1780, 1781, and 1782* . . . (2 vols., London, 1787) II, 542.

[3]Durand Echeverria, *Mirage in the West* (Princeton, 1951), 75–78, 112–13, 282–303.

[4]J. D. Say to Thomas Jefferson, received November 3, 1803, in Gilbert Chinard, *Jefferson et les ideologues* (Baltimore and Paris, 1925), 15.

when he said America was "like a youth, who from the state of a boy is growing into manhood." This adolescent gaucheness accounted for its preposterous arrogance.[5] Joseph de Maistre was more severe. "People give the example of America," he wrote. "I know nothing so exasperating," he wrote, "as the praises bestowed on that babe in swaddling clothes; wait till it grows up."[6] Harsher critics did not wait for it to grow up, for they perceived the signs of corruption and decay in the face of the infant. Thus the Irish poet, Thomas Moore, in 1803:

> Even now, in dawn of life, her sickly breath
> Burns with the taint of empires near their death,
> And, like the nymphs of her own withering clime,
> She's old in youth, she's blasted in her prime![7]

America as an infant, an adolescent, a youth was a metaphor that enjoyed a much longer life than the short-lived concept of America as a Greek colony in European usage—at least two centuries, in fact, for it has never been abandoned. It was more ambiguous, for one thing, and lent itself to quite varied uses. Late in the long history of these uses G. K. Chesterton commented on the resulting confusions. "America is always spoken of as a young nation," he wrote: "and whether or not this is a valuable and suggestive metaphor, very few people notice that it is a metaphor at all." Furthermore it was "as distracting as a mixed metaphor." It was used to mean opposite things: "something at an early stage of growth, and also something having the latest fruits of growth." It could mean a people who used chipped flints and a people who used the latest technology, and the "two meanings of youth are hopelessly mixed up when the word is applied to America." He found it "a little confusing to convey both notions by the

---

[5] Duc de La Rochefoucauld-Liancourt, *Travels Through the United States of North America* . . . (London, 1799), I, xx; II, 657.
[6] Quoted in Echeverria, *Mirage in the West*, 212.
[7] Thomas Moore, *Epistles, Odes and Other Poems* (London, 1810), 171.

same word," and declared "we must free ourselves from the talismanic tyranny of a metaphor which we do not recognize as a metaphor."[8]

Chesterton's plea went unheeded, but some of his predecessors anticipated his objections to the metaphor of youth. One of the very few major European critics to forgo it entirely was Alexis de Tocqueville. He handled the problem in part of one sentence: "The Americans are a very old and very enlightened people, who have fallen upon a new and unbounded country. . . ."[9] His contemporary Francis Grund formulated the Chestertonian ambiguity a century before Chesterton. "The Americans," he wrote, "by a singular dispensation of Providence, are enabled to profit by experience which they themselves have not made; and are enlightened by the wisdom of old age in the vigor and buoyancy of adolescence."[10] Marveling at what the country had accomplished in the Biblical three-score-and-ten-year life-span of a man, Alexander Mackay added, "But let it not be supposed that all this has been achieved in seventy years. The American republic has never had a national infancy, like that through which European nations have passed." It started full grown, "up with our own when it was first colonized."[11] The Polish writer Gurowski agreed: "America has had no childhood, no juvenility. She was not lulled at the cradle with legend, with mythic song, with the murmur of tales. The Americans matured at once, and at once wrestled with stern reality."[12]

All these may be regarded as departures from the norm, for "youth" continued firmly established as one of the standard metaphors for America among nineteenth- and twentieth-century Europeans. For the most part it was used patronizingly in some degree. For just as the metaphor of

[8] G. K. Chesterton, *What I Saw in America* (London, 1922), 196–99.
[9] Alexis de Tocqueville, *Democracy in America* (New York, 1972), II, 35.
[10] Francis J. Grund, *The Americans* (Boston, 1837), 155–56.
[11] Alexander Mackay, *The Western World* (2 vols., Philadelphia, 1849), II, 287.
[12] Adam G. Gurowski, *America and Europe* (New York, 1857), 337.

the Greek colony implied maturity, sophistication, and advanced culture, the metaphor of youth predominantly suggested immaturity, awkwardness, and irresponsibility. There seemed to be no agreement about the particular stage of youth attained, and the passage of time appears to have had no perceptible effect in determining the stage or increasing the age. The United States was a perennial youth. Oscar Wilde, in one of his inspired ironies, said, "The youth of America is their oldest tradition." Wilde erred only in attributing to America a tradition that was European in origin and in perpetuation.

In 1828, however, Karl Postl, an Austrian novelist, announced: "Their political infancy is over, they are approaching towards manhood."[13] Twenty-five years later Fredrika Bremer, the friendly Swedish critic, thought American failings and foibles of the 1850s were much like the faults of her own youth, and "may all be attributed to the youthful life of the people."[14] Another quarter-century and Sir William Howard Russell was calling the United States "a lusty youth, promising a manhood of irresistible vigour and strength in time to come if the body politic fulfils its early hope."[15] Russell's contemporary, the dour Sir Lepel Griffin, returned in 1884 to Tom Moore's image of decay in youth. "Nor can America plead youth as an excuse for her moral decrepitude," he wrote. "A vicious and depraved youth does not promise a healthy manhood or an honorable old age."[16]

The passing years did not seem to add anything to American maturity. In fact, as the twentieth century progressed, America seemed to regress in metaphorical age for Europeans. Before the First World War George Smart found

[13] Karl Postl, *The Americans As They Are, Described in a Tour Through the Valley of the Mississippi* (London, 1828), i–iii.

[14] Fredrika Bremer, *Homes of the New World* (2 vols., New York, 1853), I, 231.

[15] Sir William Howard Russell, *Hesperothen: Notes from the West: A Record of a Ramble in the United States and Canada in the Spring and Summer of 1881* (2 vols., London, 1882), I, vi.

[16] Lepel Griffin, *The Great Republic* (London, 1884), 122.

Americans "subject to the tremulousness of a youth too long continued,"[17] and Elijah Brown pronounced them "still for all intents and purposes, but the children of the world."[18] The experience of the Great War did little to alter the image. The United States emerged from it, according to a communist critic, with "the spirit of a spoilt and not very clever adolescent boy, who is unruly just for the joy of giving his seniors trouble or his juniors pain."[19] A more friendly Englishman, who married an American girl, begged Americans "without resenting it to let me regard them as children—not half way through the schools. . . ."[20] Professor C. E. M. Joad, who took delight in provoking the resentment of Americans, told them that they "do not grow up; they fail to mature," they were "still in the schoolboy stage," characterized by "a certain crudeness and immaturity of mind, a lack of mellowness and poise."[21]

There were always a few who took perverse pleasure in defying conventional wisdom and turning such established metaphors as that of American youth upside down. It was to be expected that G. K. Chesterton, in view of his warning about the mixed nature of the metaphor, provides one such example. In some ways, he thought, "America is very old indeed . . . more historic than England; I might almost say more archaeological. . . ." Just as "a pagan city is preserved at Pompeii" modern America, besides her antique postal service, preserved strata of the past "morally remote and probably irrecoverable," for example, "whole patches and particular aspects that seem to me quite Early Victorian."[22] In another sense Georges Duhamel considered "the American people older than we [Europeans], a people prematurely old perhaps, who never properly matured, but who even now are

[17] George Thomas Smart, *The Temper of the American People* (Boston, 1912), 84.
[18] Elijah Brown, *The Real America* (London, 1913), 16.
[19] W. T. Colyer, *Americanism: A World Menace* (London, 1922), 61.
[20] Moreton Frewen, *Melton Mowbray and Other Memories* (London, 1924), 197.
[21] C. E. M. Joad, *The Babbit Warren* (New York, 1927), 111–12.
[22] Chesterton, *What I Saw in America*, 200–201.

enacting for us many scenes of our future life," in material and technological aspects. [23] Another French critic, Odette Keun, dismissed "this preposterous label of 'youth'" as an excuse for American "obduracy, slackness, or irresponsibility" and immaturity, "which is not at all the same thing as youth."[24]

Youth nevertheless held its own among competitive metaphors for America. In 1947, when Europeans in their weakness following the Second World War were looking to America for vital aid, Cyril Connolly, who was not given to softness on the subject, spoke enthusiastically of "the wonderful *jeunesse* of America" whose people were "to retain their idealism, and vitality and courage and imagination into adult life" and bring salvation to Europe. [25] And finally, after much water had gone under the bridge, on the eve of the American bicentennial celebration, Constantine Doxiadis, a Greek with the perspective of his native land on the relative age of cultures, suggested that America might more appropriately celebrate its twentieth rather than its two hundredth birthday in 1976. "You will ask if you are an adolescent," he wrote. "You certainly are . . . a promising adolescent who is lost among many dreams and disappointments."[26]

In the meantime the debate continued over whether American culture was essentially different from European, the question raised by the metaphor of the Greek colony. If it were different, in what manner, what degree, and how permanently was it so? All along a few Europeans clung to some postulate of the Greek colony and emphasized similarities instead of differences. Americans, they held, were only transplanted Europeans, with a few Africans and Indian aborigines in the background. Contrasts and differences had been exag-

[23] Georges Duhamel, *America: The Menace* (New York, 1931), xiv, 203.
[24] Odette Keun, *I Think Aloud in America* (London, 1939), 255–56.
[25] Cyril Connolly, "Introduction," *Horizon*, No. 93-4 (Oct. 1947), 11.
[26] Constantine A. Doxiadis, "Three Letters to an American," *Daedalus* (Fall 1972), 175–76.

gerated. As the debate continued, however, the opposing side seemed to gain ascendancy and the testimony favoring American differences increased. From an English standpoint, Chesterton thought America "far more foreign than France or even than Ireland," with a "strangeness which marks the frontier of any fairyland." He quoted Max Beerbohm half seriously as saying, "They are as different from us as Hottentots."[27] Hilaire Belloc wrote a book entitled *The Contrast* to prove that "the New World is wholly alien to the Old." He brought to bear, he stressed, "every adjective and adverb I could use, alien, foreign, different: not Europe, not Africa, not the Old World at all. In each smallest differential of a million details The Contrast was apparent. In the integration of the whole that Contrast was overwhelming."[28]

Europeans experimented with other metaphors and analogies in their efforts to capture elusive qualities and marked differences they sensed or believed they saw in American life. Most foreign tourists visited Niagara Falls, and many were inspired to see in the spectacle the symbol they sought. They put it to varied uses. G. Lowes Dickinson went so far as to say, "All America is Niagara. . . . Force without direction, noise without significance, speed without accomplishment."[29] Writers strained their resources to express the impact of speed, mass, size, and power, the restlessness and rootlessness, and particularly what they often identified as the abstractness of American life.

To a writer of Irish origins, the American appeared to know "nothing of the ties which bind the denizen of the Old World to the home of his fathers. Patriotism with the American is not a passionate regard for its soil and its associations. It is a mere abstract notion made up of personal interest, prejudice, and pride."[30] A Norwegian in Wisconsin of the mid-

[27] Chesterton, *What I Saw in America*, 182.
[28] Hilaire Belloc, *The Contrast* (New York, 1924), 27–28, 48–50.
[29] G. Loewes Dickinson, *Appearances* (New York, 1914), 150.
[30] Thomas Holley Grattan, *Civilized America* (2 vols., London, 1859), II, 97–99.

nineteenth century found "not a single grown man or woman [who was] native to the place," and therefore no such sentiment as "in Norway binds a person to a particular locality."[31] One church spire was the same as another to an American, thought the French socialist Michel Chevalier. "The poetical associations which invest particular spots or objects with a character of sanctity, have no place in his mind."[32] The Americans revealed "little or none of the local attachments which distinguish the European," observed a Scotsman.[33] "They are an unsettled people . . . almost nomadic," wrote James Bryce. "Nobody feels rooted to the soil. Here today and gone tomorrow. . . ."[34] It was not so much democracy that distinguished American from European society as it was mobility, what the Polish journalist Adam G. Gurowski called "a devouring mobility."[35] Nor was it a temporary result of advancing frontiers, for the compulsion swept on past the frontier era. Exceeding his customary hyperbole, Belloc maintained that "in all recorded history," no people had approached such physical restlessness, "not even the nomads of Asia, still less any settled populace of the Old World."[36]

These traits very early became associated in European minds with what they perceived as a peculiar kind of national identity among Americans. There was an abstract quality about this American nationalism or patriotism that puzzled them. It was "something very different," according to Alexander MacKay, "from what is generally understood by the term." It was rather "the feeling which they cherish towards their institutions," than toward place, country, patria; "give the American his institutions, and he cares but little where

[31] Ole Munch Raeder, *America in the Forties* (Minneapolis, 1929), 148–49.
[32] Michel Chevalier, *Society, Manners and Politics in the United States* (Boston, 1839), 198.
[33] Alexander Mackay, *The Western World* (2 vols., Philadelphia, 1849), II, 288–89.
[34] James Bryce, *American Commonwealth* (2 vols., London, 1888), II, 251.
[35] Gurowski, *America and Europe*, 151.
[36] Belloc, *The Contrast*, 118–19.

you place him."[37] Places were more or less interchangeable. Americans have even been called "a people without a patria, not politically but spiritually."[38] "An American," observed a Bohemian after several years' residence, "does not love his country as a Frenchman loves France, or an Englishman loves England: America is to him but the physical means of establishing a moral power . . . 'the local habitation' of his political doctrines." The patriots *"love* their country, not, indeed, *as it is,* but *as it will be.* They do not love the land of their fathers; but . . . that which their children are destined to inherit. They live in the future, and *make* this country as they go on." He considered it a "genuine," if eccentric type of patriotism, even perhaps "the most exalted love of country" to be found.[39]

Others were doubtful that anything so abstract could provide a cement that would hold and keep the social structure from crumbling. "In the first place," wrote George Smart, "at its beginning, America was a system of ideas, a country of the soul's hope, and nothing more."[40] A people of widely varied origins and beliefs were held together by little more than a political compact. They had managed to endow their eighteenth-century constitution with a kind of sanctity. "The non-rational, transcendental cult of the Constitution is a political Principle of Life for the Americans," suggested Belloc, who thought it provided them "with exactly that kind of authority which distinguished the half-divine kingships of old."[41] Yet the whole structure was put together in the full glare of modern history for all to see.

By the twentieth century Europeans began to perceive— some dimly, some more explicitly—that the Americans had

[37] Mackay, *The Western World,* II, 288–89.
[38] C. A. Brooke-Cunningham, *Anglo-Saxon Unity and Other Essays* (London, 1925), 75.
[39] Grund, *The Americans,* 148–49, 151.
[40] Smart, *The Temper of the American People,* 13.
[41] Belloc, *The Contrast,* 129, 131.

constructed for themselves something resembling what Rousseau had called in *The Social Contract* a "civil religion." "America is a religion as no other country is," as Smart saw it, a religion that "preempts the deeper reverences of men. After years of residence one still wonders at the absorbing nature of this worship, and that a country so reverent to its abstract personifications is so irreverent to its concrete personalities."[42] It was a reverence for ideas, symbols, ceremonies, but not for people, leaders, officials. Spokesmen of the older conventional religion such as Gustaf Unonius of Sweden, more than once complained that "Citizenship in the republic became more important than citizenship in the Kingdom of God," and that "these young people seemed to take pride in showing that the blessed benefits of freedom carried with them no obligation to show obedience either to teachers or parents."[43] Nearly all Europeans who took notice of them at all, complained of the irreverence, disobedience, disrespect, and what they often ironically called the "precocity" of the young in America.

Toward the phenomenon of civil religion Europeans were inclined to be patronizing or skeptical. "Many Americans," wrote a German visitor, "with their uncomplicated simplicity, are not 'too clever' to believe in democracy . . . not 'too highly educated' to believe in political freedom . . . not 'too skeptical' to believe in political ideals in general," and were thus "willing to make sacrifices."[44] Few Europeans who gave any thought to the future of this edifice of civil religion took much stock in its durability. "Here is a something which has not grown, but was planned," wrote Belloc, from his special thirteenth-century perspective; "which took no force from the weight of the centuries . . . which has no foundation in sanctifying legend."

[42] Smart, *The Temper of the American People*, 86.
[43] *The Memoirs of Gustaf Unonius, a Pioneer in Northwest America, 1841–1856* (2 vols., Minneapolis, 1960), II, 114–15.
[44] Arthur Feiler, *America Seen Through German Eyes* (New York, 1928), 241.

He speculated further, "let this religion be weakened by a shifting of its authority to an attempted rational basis, and the American Commonwealth will dissolve."[45] Even that most hopeful foreign philosopher of the Commonwealth, James Bryce, could picture himself, "sometimes, standing in the midst of a great American city . . . marking the sharp contrasts of poverty and wealth, an increasing mass of wretchedness and an increasing display of luxury. . . ." He confessed himself to be "startled by the thought of what might befall this huge yet delicate fabric of laws and commerce and social institutions were the foundation it rested on to crumble away. Suppose all these men ceased to believe that there was any power above them, any future before them. . . ."[46] His most consoling reflection was that "free government has prospered best among religious people"—a dubious historical correlation of freedom with religiosity that he did not elaborate.

To tap the origins of another favorite European analogy for America we must turn back to the middle of the nineteenth century. Soon after the Americans had planted their flag on the Pacific coast and expanded south at the expense of a neighboring country, a new metaphor for America appeared: the United States as "The New Rome." A book of German authorship under that title was published in 1853 with the subtitle, *or, The United States of the World.*[47] The Greek colony was by this time long forgotten, and now the Roman image was put to both pejorative and laudatory uses, though they had the Empire in mind more often than the Republic. Michel Chevalier, one of the earliest to suggest it, anticipated both uses. "The Anglo-Americans," he wrote, "have much resemblance to the Romans whether for good or evil. I do not say they are destined to become the masters of the world; I merely mean to affirm that by the side of faults which shock

45 Belloc, *The Contrast*, 131.
46 Bryce, *American Commonwealth*, II, 582.
47 Theodore Poesche and Charles Goepp, *The New Rome; or the United States of the World* (New York, 1853), 111, 47.

and offend foreign nations, they have great powers and precious qualities."[48] The latter qualities predominated at mid-century in the minds of European admirers who agreed that "the future of the Anglo-American Commonwealth is pregnant with mighty destinies."[49] They compared the assurance and success with which the Americans were establishing self-governing states on the Pacific coast with the contemporaneous failures and ineptitudes of the Men of '48 in the revolutionary fiascoes of Europe. Adam G. Gurowski concluded that the American state builders "possess more constructive aptitude for organizing society than the theorists, the reformers, the leaders of the European revolutions of 1848."[50]

None of the other European admirers of the New Romans of the West could match the fervor of a champion from Bohemia. "Their political doctrines," he wrote, "have become the religion and confession of all countries, like the truths of Christianity," and were "destined to become the universal faith of mankind."[51] A Norwegian declared that the democratic republic had "become a model state for Europe," and proposed a confederation he described as "closely modeled on the American constitution," to unite the Scandinavian countries. "And what a wonderful example America gives the world," he exclaimed. "What a marvelous sight."[52] Fredrika Bremer of Sweden hailed the phenomenon enthusiastically as a revival of the Viking spirit. This new conqueror is at home on the earth," she said, "and he can turn every thing to his account. . . . He thus feels himself to be the lord of the earth . . . and is capable of accomplishing great things."[53]

A bit later even a few Englishmen were infected tempo-

[48] Chevalier, *Society, Manners and Politics*, 435–36.

[49] Mackay, *The Western World*, II, 298.

[50] Gurowski, *America and Europe*, 152–53; Poesche and Goepp, *The New Rome*, iii, 62, 177.

[51] Grund, *The Americans*, 149–50.

[52] Raeder, *America in the Forties*, 89, 207, 209.

[53] Bremer, *Homes of the New World*, I, 246–47.

rarily. Reversing the normal experience and entering the country from the west, young Rudyard Kipling married an American girl and settled in Vermont for four years. The American he encountered both appalled and astonished him. "There is nothing known to man he will not be," he wrote, "and his country will sway the world with one foot as a man tilts a seesaw plank!"[54] On a visit in 1882 Herbert Spencer announced that "the Americans may reasonably look forward to a time when they will have produced a civilization grander than any the world has known."[55] One enthusiast proposed "to constitute as one vast federated unity the English-speaking United States of the World," under American initiative.[56]

That was not at all the way the New Romans presented themselves to the predominantly conservative European mind. The American appeared more often as the Roman on the march, the empire builder and expander. "He has made maps of his empire, including all the [North American] continent," wrote Anthony Trollope, "and has preached the Monroe doctrine as though it had been decreed by the gods. He has told the world of his increasing millions. . . . He has boasted aloud in his pride, and called on all men to look at his glory."[57] He was even looking across the Atlantic to Europe with fantasies of playing Rome to a declining Greece. Americans were firmly and repeatedly informed that this role was not for them. "The democratic forms of America are widely inconsistent with the instincts, traditions, and capabilities of the European nations," declared a British diplomat, and he pointed to the failure of the revolutions of 1848 and later and "their miserable result" as proof.[58] To Sir Lepel Griffin it was clear that "no greater curse could befall England than for her

[54] Rudyard Kipling, *American Notes* (New York, n.d.), 192–93.
[55] E. L. Youmans, *Herbert Spencer on the Americans* . . . (New York, 1883), 19–20.
[56] W. T. Stead, *The Americanization of the World* (New York, 1901), 397.
[57] A. Trollope, *North America*, II, 239.
[58] Grattan, *Civilized America*, I, xiii.

to borrow political methods, dogmas and institutions from America."[59]

The Roman metaphor for America enjoyed some periodic revival among twentieth-century Europeans given to dwelling on America's premature decadence, decline, and moral degeneration.[60] Less was heard of Rome, however, after Lord Bryce found wanting various historical analogies he examined, including the relation of "Rome to Greece in the second and third centuries before Christ" and that of "northern and Western Europe to Italy in the fifteenth." He decided that "no historical parallel can be found."[61] Hilaire Belloc later agreed that "judgment based upon such apparent parallels misleads us altogether."[62] But the Roman analogy was never entirely abandoned. The bleak postwar year of 1947 found Cyril Connolly writing: "As Europe becomes more helpless the Americans are compelled to become far-seeing and responsible, as Rome was forced by the long decline of Greece to produce an Augustus, a Virgil. *Our impotence liberates their potentialities.*"[63]

When Europeans spoke of America as the land of the future as many of them did from time to time, they usually meant Europe's future, and they had many things in mind, often quite irreconcilable things. Had they combined to present to the United States a statue personifying this Future, as France had presented her a statue of Liberty, they would never have agreed on what aspect the personification should wear. Whether they saw a darker or a brighter vision, America-watchers of Europe were agreed that portents of the future were to be read there—perhaps even the future itself.

[59] Griffin, *The Great Republic*, 3, 6.
[60] For example, Huxley, *Jesting Pilate*, 267–68; and Joad, *The Babbit Warren*, *passim*.
[61] Bryce, *American Commonwealth*, II, 634–37.
[62] Belloc, *The Contrast*, 233–34.
[63] Connolly, "Introduction," 11.

With his usual detachment, Tocqueville read the future without cheers and without tears. He wrote his book on America, he said "with a mind constantly occupied by a single thought—that the advent of democracy as a governing power in the world's affairs, universal and irresistible, was at hand." He tells us explicitly "with what intention" he undertook the "question here discussed," and how "it concerns, not a nation only, but all mankind." Democracy he regarded as the fate of mankind and that fate was being rehearsed in America. His more perceptive contemporaries read him that way. John Stuart Mill recommended the book as "all the more worthy of study in that it harbors within its depths the future of the world."[64]

Others were not so sure about the inevitability of democracy or so persuaded about the importance of democracy and equality in making America the way it was, though they might still believe that hers was the way of the future. James Bryce thought many forces were at work and doubted that democracy was the most important of them. Yet like Tocqueville he also believed that much of Europe's future could be read in American experience. "America has in some respects anticipated European nations," he wrote. "She is walking before them along a path which they may probably follow. She carries behind her, to adopt a famous simile of Dante's, a lamp whose light helps those who come after her more than it always does herself. . . ." He pointed to a number of examples and added that "nothing can be more instructive than American experience," if Europe rightly read it.[65]

Europeans gradually adjusted, some with composure, some with resignation, to the older view of America as the future. Discounting the visions of enthusiasts who saw America as a utopia realized or optimism justified, they accepted

[64] Tocqueville, *Democracy in America*, I, xxiv, 326; Marvin Zetterbaum, *Tocqueville and the Problem of Democracy* (Stanford, 1967), 16.
[65] Bryce, *American Commonwealth*, II, 475–80.

what they saw as admonition about the future—blunders and mistakes to be avoided, inevitabilities to be prepared for, blind forces to be guided. So conceived, America as the land of the future was a remote barometer to be watched for what to expect rather than a force to be resisted as an intruding influence.

Then the future began to arrive in the present. It arrived at the Europeans' doorstep, their markets, their press, their schools. It arrived in the shape of investments, new foods, industrial products, machines, gadgets. The future intruded in the shape of missionaries, evangelists, salesmen, advertisements, and movies. It took the form of new brides in the oldest of families, new faces in the highest society. It also appeared at lower social levels in strange attitudes and ideas, new ways of thinking, new styles of living, and alien values. Europeans began to hear these innovations from the mouths of their own children and with increasing apprehension and dismay. The future was no longer a remote transatlantic barometer or a flickering image on a distant Screen in the West. The future was an intrusive, unavoidable, living presence. They called it "Americanization."

Here and there, but mainly in Britain, were those who could accept this future of the present without deep concern, even welcome it. One English spokesman early in the twentieth century urged his countrymen to "contemplate with satisfaction and even with enthusiasm the Americanization of the world," since it was "but the Anglicanization of the world at one remove" and should be properly regarded as "the greatest achievement of our race."[66] That was by no means a widely accepted view even in Britain, where "an Americanized England" was described by a more typical phrase as "a serious menace." What Britain had offered the world, it was said, was a benign Hellenization, not the Roman-style Ameri-

[66] Stead, *The Americanization of the World*, 2, 4, 161.

canization which "seems destined to swallow up Europe" and should be resisted at all costs.[67]

From other countries of Europe—the more advanced the earlier and the louder—came the cry against Americanization—from France, from Germany, from the Scandinavian countries, from Austria and Italy. In 1899, the Pope explicitly condemned "Americanism" as a doctrine at variance with established beliefs. The impact on life was variously perceived as depersonalization, standardization, mechanization, a transvaluation of all traditional values. The transformations by the 1930s were seen either in progress or in immediate prospect and they were strongly associated with America. A German writer in 1929 had it that "America today determines, in a representative manner, the style of life of the whole Euramerican world," that "the whole of our civilization is becoming more and more Americanized," and that "no one can deny the fact that when we gaze across the ocean we behold the image of our own future, as though in a magic mirror." He was sure that no previous world conquest "can compare with that of Americanization in extent or effectiveness."[68]

A curious feature of such pronouncements on Americanization is that they often disavow concrete reference to America itself. Thus the German just quoted immediately added: "I am writing, therefore, not really about America . . . but about that 'idea' which is, of course, conditioned by the concrete America, but which as an abstraction has already made itself felt throughout the world . . . an abstract reality which expresses itself in millions of ways, in men and in things, but never appears in a perfectly 'pure'

[67]Brown, *The Real America*, 150, 163; Dickinson, *Appearances*, 201; C. H. Bretherton, *Midas or The United States and the Future* (New York, 1926), 16.

[68]Richard Müller Freienfels, *Mysteries of the Soul* (London, 1929), 239, 287.

form."[69] Another example, a little later, comes from Georges Duhamel. Toward the end of his book, *America: The Menace,* we suddenly encounter this paragraph: "America? I am not talking of America. By means of this America I am questioning the future; I am trying to determine the path that, willy-nilly, we [that is, Europeans] must follow." As for the Americans themselves, he said, they "seem to me like pure ideograms, like the signs of an abstract, algebraic, and yet already fabulous civilization."[70]

Looking back over our survey of metaphors by which Europeans have conceived of and represented America since the eighteenth century, we see that a transformation has taken place not merely in the forms and images but in the character and purpose of the metaphor itself. We started with the metaphor America as Republican Rome; then on to America as a Greek colony; later we encountered America as Imperial Rome, America as adolescent, as perennial youth, and America as the Land of the Future. But these were all metaphors *for* America, ways of conceiving *of* America. What we finally encounter in talk of the Americanization of Europe is the use of America *as* a metaphor, a way of thinking about what is happening to Europe. Tocqueville had anticipated the purpose and method in his study, as he confessed in a letter to John Stuart Mill: "America was only my framework; *democratie* was the subject."[71] But this was not quite the same as using America *as* a metaphor. That is a modern usage.

The more candid of the modern users admitted that one of the chief horrors of Americanization was that for the most part the European masses embraced it eagerly, that it represented more or less what they wanted. Some of the deplorers of Americanization also admitted that the transformations they

[69] Ibid., 240.
[70] Duhamel, *America: The Menace,* 191, 42.
[71] Quoted in George W. Pierson, *Tocqueville and Beaumont in America* (New York, 1938), 748.

abhorred were the products of internal rather than external forces, universal and impersonal forces producing phenomena that would have taken place without American influence. That did not matter to an embattled elite desperately defending European traditions against subversion by modernism, nor did it matter to a subversive elite seeking overthrow of those traditions for revolutionary ends. Both found America as metaphor adapted to their uses. Ignazio Silone has a character say in his *Fontamara*, "America's everywhere. All you need is to have eyes to see it."[72] Any resemblance to historical or geographic or social realities was purely coincidental. But that had been as true of the historical metaphors *for* America as it was of America *as* metaphor.

The making of metaphors *for* America, however, shows no signs of disappearing and continues to flourish alongside its modern use *as* a metaphor. Undiscouraged by his observation that so little had changed in America during the last two centuries and so much has already been said and repeated, the modern French sociologist Jean Baudrillard, cited earlier, perseveres in the conviction that "the truth of America can only be seen by a European." Among our gleanings of alien corn his contributions stand out with a certain typological perfection. After borrowing a number of well-worn clichés from earlier European truth seers, he pushes on to contemporary Hollywood in a search for fresh sources and inspirations. On the assumption that "the whole of the Western world is hypostatized in America, the whole of America in California, and California in MGM and Disneyland," it follows that Disneyland is "the microcosm of the West,"[73] Microcosm is not quite the same as metaphor, but it is pretty near.

[72] Ignazio Silone, *Fontamara*, tr. Eric Mosbacher (London, 1985), 35.
[73] Jean Baudrillard, *America* (New York, 1988), 55.

5

Russo-American
Counterpoint

Up TO THIS POINT we have singled out no one European
nation for special attention in speaking of Old World opinions
and images of America. There would seem to be reason,
however, for making one exception to the rule, and the reason
is provided by a practice to which some Europeans have long
been habituated. In looking westward for portents of what the
future promised or threatened, Europeans often turned back
to look over their shoulders eastward for promises and threats
from the opposite direction. The Russo-American comparison was irresistible for Europeans. It was difficult to say
whether they were more fascinated by the differences or the
similarities. Some looked to one country for hope, some to the
other; some found one a menace, some the other, and a few
found menaces in both Russia and America.

The most often quoted, though by no means the first
formulation of the comparison, was that with which Tocqueville concluded the first part of his *Democracy in America* in
1835:

There are at the present time two great nations in the world, which started from different points, but seem to tend towards the same end. I allude to the Russians and the Americans. Both of them have grown up unnoticed; and while the attention of mankind was directed elsewhere, they have suddenly placed themselves in the front rank among nations, and the world learned their existence and their greatness at almost the same time.

All other nations seem to have nearly reached their natural limits, and they have only to maintain their power; but these are still in the act of growth. All the others have stopped or continue to advance with extreme difficulty; these alone are proceeding with ease and celerity along a path to which no limit can be perceived.[1]

Among the first to open the long history of Russo-American counterpoint were apparently the Russians and Americans themselves. Crèvecœur quotes a letter from a Russian gentleman who had spent four years in America during the last quarter of the eighteenth century: "the Russians may be in some respects compared to you," he said; "we likewise are a new people, new I mean in knowledge, arts, and improvements. Who knows what revolutions Russia and America may one day bring about; we are perhaps nearer neighbours than we imagine. . . . The foundation of thy civil polity must lead thee in a few years to a degree of population and power which Europe little thinks of!"[2] An American writer, Alexander H. Everett, secretary to John Quincy Adams during his mission in Russia, found it in 1827 "an almost miraculous concurrence of events" that while his fellow countrymen "were appropriating to themselves the boundless regions of the new world, the Czars of Russia were stretching their jurisdiction over equally extensive territories,

---

[1] Alexis de Tocqueville, *Democracy in America* (New York, 1972), I, 434.
[2] J. Hector St. John de Crèvecœur, *Letters from an American Farmer* (London, 1912), 184, 187. The Russian visitor is cryptically identified as "Mr. Iw—n Al—z."

which being contiguous to their former possessions, were not liable to fall off."[3] Americans continued to compare themselves with Russians. In 1881 Walt Whitman exclaimed, "You Russians and we Americans! Our countries are so distant, so unlike at first glance—such a distance . . . and yet in certain features, and vaster ones, so resembling each other."[4]

Before Tocqueville's book appeared, a common topic of conversation in St. Petersburg was the possibility that some day the United States and Russia might dominate Europe politically and intellectually. Some even fancied they found a parallel between the democratic equality of the Americans and the general leveling of society the Romanovs had accomplished in Russia.[5]

No passing fad, the Russo-American antithesis gained a permanent place on the agenda of the international community of intellectuals. It varied over the years in prominence and in the numerous and often conflicting political purposes made of it, but it has remained available and useful to many thinkers throughout the last two centuries and into our own time. A German scholar who has sketched its history in Europe as a means of defining Western identity has called it *"die grosse Parallele."* He stresses the twentieth century, but he goes back to Napoleon on St. Helena saying that the future of the world lay either in the American or the Russian way, and comes on down to Spengler and Toynbee.[6] Given the prominence

    [3] Alexander Hill Everett, *America: A General Survey of the Political Situation of the Several Powers of the Western Continent, with Conjectures on Their Future Prospects* (Philadelphia, 1827), 16, 23, 35.

    [4] Whitman to John Fitzgerald Lee, Dublin, Dec. 20, 1881, in Edwin H. Miller, ed., *Correspondence of Walt Whitman* (3 vols., New York, 1964), III, 259. Whitman apologized for addressing the Irishman, who wanted to translate his poetry into Russian, as if he were a Russian.

    [5] A. J. Thurston, "Alexis de Tocqueville in Russia," *Journal of the History of Ideas* 37 (1976): 338–39.

    [6] Dieter Groh, *Russland und das Selbstverstandnis Europas* (Neuwied, 1961), 137–39, 166, 171–79; see also Bertrand Fabian, *Alexis de Tocquevilles Americabild* (Heidelberg, 1957), 80–108, esp. 101–2; and also John Gould Fletcher, *Europe's Two Frontiers* (London, 1930).

of this theme, there would seem to be plenty of reason for singling out Russia, not only for attention to the American comparison, but for distinctive West European perceptions of Russia, as well as distinctive Russian perceptions of America.

In addressing the Russo-American comparison, even the more circumspect and profound West Europeans were prone to permit cultural or political bias to warp their generalizations. The most prominent of them, Tocqueville was uncharacteristically rash in parts of the famous passage following that quoted above. In advancing their respective frontiers, he said,

> The American struggles against the obstacles that nature opposes to him; the adversaries of the Russian are men. . . . The conquests of the American are therefore gained by the plowshare; those of the Russian by the sword. The Anglo-American relies upon personal interest to accomplish his ends and gives free scope to the unguided strength and common sense of the people; the Russian centers all the authority of society in a single arm. The principal instrument of the former is freedom; of the latter, servitude. Their starting-point is different and their courses are not the same; yet each of them seems marked out by the will of Heaven to sway the destinies of half the globe.[7]

The inspired young prophet and seer seems to have momentarily forgotten the roles that the red Indian and the black slave played in the drama of American conquest—the one in resisting, the other in advancing its march. In light of later events we must also take exception to the concluding phrases about "the will of God" and "the destinies of half the globe." As striking as it is as an anticipation of ambitions sometimes held in both nations, there was nothing in 1835 foreordained, predestined, or inevitable about the outcome.

Two years later, in 1837, Grund far outdid Tocqueville

[7] Tocqueville, *Democracy in America*, I, 484.

both in the shrillness of his rhetoric and the direfulness of his prophecy. He went so far as to declare that:

Russia is the evil genius of history; while America is its guardian angel. The power of Russia is opposed to the interests of humanity; that of the United States is based on wisdom and justice. . . . The power of Russia rests on bayonets; that of America on the superiority of mind over brute force. They are to each other as darkness to light. . . . The day of battle must come; the war of principles must ensue. . . .[8]

Numerous Europeans prophesied an eventual confrontation. Two German authors as early as the 1850s agreed that "the lines are drawn. The choices are marshalled on each wing of the world's stage, Russia leading the one, the United States the other. Yet the world is too small for both, and the contest must end in the downfall of the one and the victory of the other. . . . Russia has expended all her forces in making a formidable display on her Western border. The United States is already digging trenches for an attack in the rear."[9]

From a Scandinavian point of view in the 1840s, on the other hand, there was a certain uneasiness about what appeared to be a growing bond between these monsters to the east and west. A Norwegian could not tell

whether it is a case of attraction between unlikes . . . or whether they are united in their common dislike for Great Britain. In any case there certainly seems to be a bond of sympathy between these two gigantic nations, each of which appears to be engaged in swallowing an entire continent. One hears [in America] very little criticism of the tyrannical Czar, and he is said to be particularly fond of the Americans and has many of them in his employ. Two of them are at the head of a gigantic factory in St. Petersburg, which makes locomotives and cars for the North Russian Railway.

8 Francis J. Grund, The Americans, in Their Moral, Social, and Political Relations (Boston, 1837), 392–93.

9 Theodore Poesche and Charles Goepp, The New Rome; or the United States of the World (New York, 1853), 109.

Both Americans and Russians seemed to think Europe in decline, but he notes that Americans "make an exception of one nation—Russia."[10]

From several European standpoints, mainly conservative, there seemed little to choose between the two, for the menace of barbarism seemed to loom in the west as well as in the east. For some that of the east seemed somewhat more preferable for being undisguised. The Irish Tory poet Thomas Moore put the latter view into verse in 1810:

> Oh! Freedom, freedom, how I hate thy cant!
> Not Eastern bombast, nor the savage rant
> Of purple madmen, were they numbered all
> From Roman Nero down to Russian Paul,
> Could grate upon my ear so mean, so base
> As the rank jargon of that factious race.[11]

Another Irish opinion had it that there was no more freedom (if as much) in America than in Russia, for "the tyranny of the majority, that most intolerant and bigoted of all tyrannies, rules America with a rod of iron."[12] To a French woman of like mind, it was all a matter of "the *canaille* having the right to vote." To her, "Russia, after this, should be considered a political paradise, for there but one master is to be obeyed, whilst in the United States the authority of cliques of the most opposite and shameful influences and objects must be submitted to." She pronounced the American pose of freedom "the greatest falsehood of the age."[13]

Among the more extreme positions of the sort, that of Sir Lepel Griffin stands out prominently. With the exception of Russia he believed there was "no country where private right

---

[10] Ole Munch Raeder, *America in the Forties* (Minneapolis, 1929), 88.

[11] Thomas Moore, *Epistles, Odes, and Other Poems* (London, 1810), 174–75.

[12] Edward Sullivan, *Rambles and Scrambles in North and South America* (London, 1853), 193–94.

[13] Mme. M. de Grandfort, *The New World*, tr. Edward C. Wharton (New Orleans, 1855), 43, 120.

and public interests are more systematically outraged than in the United States." And yet he stoically concluded that within a generation or two "there will be but three Great Powers in the civilised world," Great Britain, Russia, and the United States. Which made it all the more important to come to terms with "the scum of Europe which the Atlantic has washed up on the shores of the New World."[14]

Fortunately there were European views more flattering to each of the poles of comparison. In 1851 Lady Emmaline Stuart-Wortley believed that "Russia and the United States are the two young, growing, giant nations of the world—the Leviathans of the lands! . . . Those two grand young nations are strong to the race, and fresh to the glorious contest. . . . What to other nations may be work and labour, to them is but, as it were, healthful relaxation . . . the conscious enjoyment of their own inexhaustible vitality."[15] And on the eve of the First World War, Stephen Graham, who wrote on both countries and quite extensively on Russia, went further in saying that,

> Russia and America are the Eastern and Western poles of thought. Russia is evolving as the greatest artistic, philosophical and mystical nation of the world, and Moscow may be said already to be the literary capital of Europe. America is showing itself as the site of the New Jerusalem, the place where a nation is really in earnest in its attempt to realise the great dream of human progress. Russia is the living East; America is the living West. . . .[16]

The October Revolution and the new Soviet order most often had the effect of politicizing and polemicizing the uses that West Europeans made of the old Russo-American antitheses. Whereas in pre-revolutionary years these had been largely thought of as cultural, they were now perceived to be

[14]Lepel Griffin, The Great Republic (London, 1884), 2, 7, 94.
[15]Emmaline Charlotte Elizabeth Stuart-Wortley, Travels in the United States, 1849–1850 (London, 1851), 72.
[16]Stephen Graham, With Poor Immigrants to America (New York, 1914), xi.

ideological—polar opposites in ideology. European radicals tended to embrace the Soviet Union as the indispensable ally for the future establishment of socialist states in Western Europe and pictured America as the leading opponent of their hopes. The Soviet Union was now the Promised Land of Socialism, and Europeans were said to face an unavoidable choice. As the British labor leader Tom Mann put it, "if we refuse to travel towards Communism, the only alternative is to become Americanized, with all that this involves," and from his point of view all that alternative involved was quite undesirable. From the position of West European Communists, a showdown between the polar opposites was inevitable. As one of them wrote in 1922, "the world stage is now being cleared for a decisive struggle between Americanism and Communism," and the former he described as "A World Menace."[17]

While conservative and non-radical Europeans generally reversed this order of preferences, identified with America, and regarded it as the polar opposite of Soviet Russia, a considerable number of West European intellectuals persisted in stressing similarities between the embattled giants, whatever their ideological contretemps. "The resemblance to Bolshevik Russia," wrote Oswald Spengler, referring to America, "is far greater than one imagines. . . . And there is the same dictatorship there as in Russia (it does not matter that it is imposed by society instead of a party), affecting everything . . . that in the Western world [of Europe] is left to the option of individuals. There is one standardized type of American. . . . Finally, there is an almost Russian form of State socialism or State capitalism, represented by the mass of trusts."[18] Count Hermann Keyserling remarked upon "the extraordinary likeness between Bolshevik Russia and America," about the same time. "The difference actually amounts

[17] W. T. Colyer, *Americanism: A World Menace* (London, 1922), xi, 2.
[18] Oswald Spengler, *The Hour of Decision* (New York, 1929), 68.

to a mere difference in language: the spirit is the same, whatever the causes. . . . Both countries are basically socialistic. But America expresses its socialism in the form of general prosperity, and Russia in the form of general poverty."[19]

Bertrand Russell had his doubts about some of the alleged polarities; Arnold Toynbee thought the main differences between the two nations were moral rather than economic, while G. D. H. Cole believed "the essential difference" was political.[20] Denis de Rougemont held that "from the spiritual standpoint both the U.S.S.R. and the U.S.A. are regressive," and that Europe "alone possesses, in my view, the receipt for balance."[21] Whatever their differences over Russo-American contrasts or similarities, a strong if tacit conviction prevailed that West European civilization was preferable to either the American or the Russian deviation. The evidence of this cultural bias as well as for leanings to the east or the west is to be found in what West Europeans wrote over the centuries about the two countries. Enough has already been said about their response to the New World. Their reflections on Russia are too extensive to permit more than a meager sample here. Instructive collections of European writings on Muscovites and their rulers from Ivan the Terrible to the formidable Paul I by their western contemporaries are available to those interested.[22] We shall confine our samples to two mid-nineteenth writers, the Marquis Astolph de Custine of France and the Baron August von Haxthausen of Germany. They are chosen for contrast and intrinsic interest rather than for typicality, though both illustrate important countervailing themes.

Born to one of the great noble families of France in 1790,

[19] Hermann Keyserling, *America Set Free* (New York, 1929), 252–53.
[20] Edward W. Chester, *Europe Views America* (Washington, 1962), 76.
[21] Denis de Rougemont, *Man's Western Quest: The Principle of Civilization* (New York, 1957), 165.
[22] For example, Anthony Cross, ed., *Russia Under Western Eyes, 1517–1825* (London, 1971); and Peter Putnam, ed., *Seven Britons in Imperial Russia, 1698–1812* (Princeton, 1952).

Custine grew up in the shadow of the guillotine, which took the lives of his grandfather, his father, and came near taking the life of his adored mother. He made his tour of Russia in the summer of 1839, a journey that came between the publication of the first and that of the second part of Tocqueville's already famous book on America, though Custine's *La Russie en* 1839 was not published until 1843. In his perceptive study of Custine and his book, George F. Kennan has remarked upon "a strange sort of symmetry," a symmetry of similarities and opposites, "between the persons and the journeys of Custine and Tocqueville, within the same decade, to the two great developing outposts of European Civilization: Russia and America." Both men were products of aristocratic family and tradition that suffered under the Terror, and both were at odds with a declining French aristocracy and a rising social equality. They sought alternatives at opposite ends of the world and returned with answers both different and similar. Custine admired, envied, and at least once casually met Tocqueville. He also, without notable success, emulated him. He had not been very successful as a poet, a novelist, or a dramatist, but gained considerable fame for his book on Russia. While it falls short of the example he emulated and was full of factual inaccuracies and other defects, the book is nevertheless highly interesting and provocative. Alexander Herzen went so far as to say it was the best book on Russia ever written by a foreigner, and despaired to reflect that no Russian could have done it.[23]

Custine focused his attention on one important side of Russia of 1839—the side of official power and cynicism—and came down with crushingly harsh criticism upon that, while neglecting more appealing sides. He did see "the gentleness, politeness, and pacific humour of the people," but declared them to be "actuated by fear to a degree that urges them to dissimulate," knowing that the "true tyrant likes to be sur-

[23] George F. Kennan, *The Marquis de Custine and His Russia in* 1839 (Princeton, 1971), vii, 18–19, 22–23.

rounded by smiles."[24] Nothing could be trusted. "Everything is founded on appearance in Russia, whence it is that everything inspires mistrust." He rather admired Nicholas I for his skill in the role of tyrant and enjoyed talking with him as "the only man in the empire with whom one may talk without fear of informers." Fear suffused the whole order, "one single sentiment—that of fear." With it went obsession with secrecy, espionage, intimidation, and rewriting history. Oppression spread downward through all ranks from elite to serf. "I believe that in no part of the world do the men enjoy less real happiness than in Russia," he wrote. The happy peasants were pure myth. For them it was "tranquility or the knout!—this is for them the condition of existence."[25] No aspect of the system was overlooked in this terrible indictment: "A degraded brutality in the army—terror around the administration, a terror shared by even those who govern—servility in the church— hypocrisy in the nobility—ignorance and misery among the people—and Siberia for them all." He concluded on the final page with this advice for his French readers: "If ever your sons should be discontented with France, try my recipe; tell them to go to Russia. It is a useful journey for every foreigner: whoever has well examined that country will be content to live anywhere else."[26]

Among things Custine missed was the great Russian era already incipient during his visit. This was the coming period of change and reform, the foundations for local self-government, a parliamentary system, and on top of this the great flowering in literature, music, drama, and intellectual life that placed Russia on an elevation never reached before— or after. Pointing this out, George Kennan wonders "what to make of this anomaly: that the nightmare of 1839 should have become the reality of 1939," and concludes that even if

[24] Marquis de Custine, *Empire of the Czar; A Journey Through Eternal Russia* (New York, 1989), 275, 306.
[25] Ibid., 159, 203, 233, 498.
[26] Ibid., 451, 619.

Custine wrote what was "not a very good book about Russia in 1839," it has turned out to be "an excellent book, probably in fact the best of books, about the Russia of Joseph Stalin, and not a bad book about the Russia of Brezhnev and Kosygin."[27]

A comparison of Custine and his book on Russia with Haxthausen and his work is largely a matter of contrasts. While both were born to old families of the aristocracy, the German only two years after the Frenchman, and though Haxthausen followed his predecessor to Russia four years later, in 1843, the year Custine's book was published, the parallels between the two ended there. No habitué of Parisian salons, the Baron was a provincial Westphalian landholder of scholarly interests, strong conservative leanings, and religious convictions. Caught up in Romantic currents of his time, he was a traditionalist and an anti-rationalist with mystic theories about the land and man's relationship to it. His friends the famous brothers Grimm encouraged his interest in peasant life, culture, folklore, story, and song. Along with publications on these subjects, Haxthausen began serious study and writings on peasant communal institutions and agriculture in Slavic lands where he hoped his ideas would find more favorable reception than they had at home. In a widely printed essay of 1842 he praised a *ukaz* of the tsarist government putting land at the disposal of peasants while protecting landholders' rights. This brought a note of congratulations from Czar Nicholas I and an invitation to visit Russia. By the time the visitor arrived the next year the Czar was outraged by Custine's book and looking for some way to overcome the image of his empire it was broadcasting in Europe. With this in mind, Nicholas agreed to back his visitor's research and pay the costs of publication in French and German, in addition to providing him with an interpreter, a court coachman, and a supply wagon for him and an assistant during six months of field work. His enthusiasm for all things Russian won the

[27] Kennan, *The Marquis de Custine*, 124–25, 128–29.

affections of slavophiles and quieted endemic suspicions of all foreign curiosity that Custine had sharpened. [28]

Haxthausen quickly left the Petersburg courts that had fascinated Custine and plunged into the countryside "to observe and study directly the life of the so-called lower classes"—the peasants, with "unprejudiced eye," forgetting "everything he had read about it." He promised at the outset, however, that he "always observed with love, for he has always stood in awe of all genuine, vigorous, and untainted popular institutions!"[29] And what could be more genuine and untainted than the Russian commune! The Baron was at times carried away with awe and enthusiasm for the organic unity, hierarchy, and patriarchy of it all, embracing serf, landowner, lord, and czar in one order under God. He found that "serfdom was not very oppressive for the true peasants," and that "pure self-interest forced the master to be gentle, considerate, and helpful to his peasants." He told of one master, his host during an extended visit, who "enjoyed the same love and respect" of his serfs wherever he went, and indeed, he asked, "Who could look into his gentle, friendly eyes and not be convinced that his heart was imbued only with the purest love of humanity!"[30] They called him father. In fact the typical Russian "designates God, the tsar, the priest, and every old man as father and calls the church his mother," not to mention Mother Volga, Mother Moscow, and Holy Mother Russia. "He loves the authoritarianism of a father. . . . He demands that his superiors be firm. . . . He loves human arbitrariness." The serf did "not consider it a punishment but a blessing to be sent to Siberia" by a stern master. The Czar was "absolutely essential" to the system and Russian society would "cease to exist without the tsar," for "the tsar can never err, in the people's opinion." The system also made revolution-

[28] August von Haxthausen, *Studies on the Interior of Russia,* ed. S. Frederick Starr, with an Introduction (Chicago, 1972), vii–xx.
[29] Ibid., 3, 8.
[30] Ibid., 43–44, 72, 75, 82–83.

ary overthrow of the government unthinkable in Russia.[31]

Publication of the Baron's findings did not begin until 1849, but the timing could hardly have been improved from several points of view. European radicals, battered and defeated in the revolutions of 1848, could find comfort in learning from Haxthausen that the theories for which they fought under "the general name of communism and socialism" were alive and well and living in Russia, where the communes "obviously bear an outward similarity to the utopias which those theories seek to create in western Europe." Radicals rained praise on him for discovering Russia and its home-grown communalism. Conservatives, for their part, were hardly less grateful to him for proof that social felicity and harmony could be realized under traditional institutions and for hope that reunion of Greek Orthodoxy with the Holy See of Rome might instill the Christian piety of the Russians into western Catholicism. It was not surprising that a Russian diplomat should conclude that "the existence of this man is an advantage for us." It is more surprising to find Alexander Herzen, who had praised Custine's book, now declaring that "Haxthausen is completely right," and the revolutionist Nikolai Chernyshevski echoing him.[32]

In view of the special character of attention Europeans have given Russia and the uses they made of it; in view of their old habit of coupling Russia with America for comparative purposes; and because of a consequent sharpening of Russian perception of America, we would surely seem justified in differentiating Russian opinion of the New World and giving it separate attention. While it differed in several ways, Russian opinion like that of other countries was strongly influenced by current diplomatic relations as they changed over the years. We can do no more here than refer in passing to major periods and give a few examples from each. The first and longest

[31] Ibid., 191, 282, 285–88, 290, 292.
[32] Ibid., 92; and Starr in Introduction, xxix–xxxv.

period, that from the American Revolution to 1867, has been called by an American diplomatic historian "A Heritage of Harmony," and the standard history of the first forty years of that long period is provided by the Russian historian Nikolai N. Bolkhovitinov.[33]

The most impassioned Russian supporter of transatlantic freedom was the revolutionist Alexander Radischev, whose writings in Bolkhovitinov's opinion "belong among the outstanding responses in world literature to the American Revolution."[34] Radischev was not wholly uncritical of the Americans, for he reproved them for their continuation of African slavery and their denial of Indian rights. Nevertheless his ode to "Liberty" in 1783 rang with eloquent enthusiasm for the revolution in the New World and one to come in the Old World:

> O glorious land,
> Where once freedom lay trampled,
> Bent under the yoke.
> Thou rejoiceth now, while we still suffer!
> We all thirst for the same things.
> Thy example has revealed the goal.

Both nations were quite aware of the ideological gulf that separated them, yet common enemies and national self-interest served to bridge the gulf for some remarkable exchanges. Most notable was the cordial correspondence between the young and the initially liberal Czar Alexander I and President Thomas Jefferson. Alexander once spoke of the United States as "so wise and so well-governed," and Jefferson bordered on the lavish in compliments to the young Czar. An

[33] John Lewis Gaddis, *Russia, the Soviet Union, and the United States: An Interpretive History* (New York, 1978), 1–26; Nikolai N. Bolkhovitinov, *The Beginnings of Russian-American Relations, 1775–1815*, tr. Elena Levin (Cambridge, Mass., 1975).
[34] Bolkhovitinov, *The Beginnings*, 47, 52, 54.

American historian, wondering "how two such ideologically disparate states could get along with each other as well as they did," points to the congruence of interests between them during the Napoleonic wars that obscured potential areas of conflict.[35] After all, while Russians were sifting the ashes of Moscow after the retreat of Napoleon in 1812, Americans were simultaneously sifting the ashes of a Washington put to the torch by English invaders. Paul Svenin, a member of the first Russian diplomatic mission to the United States, wrote in 1813, with rather more diplomacy than realism, that "No two countries bear a more striking resemblance than Russia and the United States. . . . In Russia, as in the United States, the unfortunate and the persecuted find an asylum and a home. . . . It is hoped that frequent intercourse now existing will facilitate the knowledge of these two countries, and unite them still more closely."[36] Americans looked to Russia as a counterweight to Britain and France, and Russians were grateful for American sympathy during the Crimean War. One manifestation of their gratitude was their sympathetic neutrality toward the Union cause during the American Civil War and the dispatch of both Atlantic and Pacific fleets to winter in U.S. ports in 1863. This followed hard upon the drama of serf emancipation in Russia and slave emancipation in America.

It was not from official or government sources that pro-American writings flowed, however, but from opponents of the government, most often from revolutionary opponents in exile. American ideals, liberties, and constitutional principles inspired the ill-starred Decembrist Revolutionsts of 1825. According to one of them, "the North American States filled the minds of Russian youth at that time" and inspired "their independent mode of life and their democratic political order." Not they, however, but their younger successors who

---

[35] Gaddis, *Russia, the Soviet Union, and the United States*, 12, 17, 20–22.
[36] Paul Svenin, *Sketches of Moscow and St. Petersburg* (Philadelphia, 1813), 2.

vowed to avenge them and realize or radicalize their revolutionary goals, are the ones who left the most complete account
of their feelings about America. Utopians and pre-Marxist
socialists, this generation reached its crisis and turning point
in 1848, year of crushed revolutions, and spent the mid-
century years and beyond explaining and rationalizing the past
and plotting the future.[37]

More perhaps than any of his comrades and rivals of that
generation, Alexander Herzen looked to America for hope,
encouragement, and consolation. He was aware of American
faults and could be harshly critical of them, but he believed
them outweighed by her virtues. He knew there were fundamental differences between the two cultures, but he cherished
the belief that they had common meeting points of value to
both and that his people had much to gain from the example of
American democracy. The two cultures were "opposite but
incomplete" and should "complement rather than exclude
each other." Herzen never visited America, but once said that
"if I were not a Russian, I should long ago have gone away to
America," and in 1851 declared that for a free man there was
"no other refuge in Europe than the deck of a vessel making
sail for America." He remained emphatically persuaded that
"Russia has but one comrade and travelling companion for the
future—the United States."[38]

Lines of agreement and disagreement on America ran
back and forth between Herzen and his radical friends and
associates. His lifelong poet friend Nicholai Ogarev outdid
him as a pro-American, while his stormy comrade Mikhail
Bakunin mixed exorbitant praise with severe criticism. Escap-

[37] Anatole G. Mazour, *The First Russian Revolution: 1825; The Decembrist Movement, Its Origins, Development, and Significance* (Stanford, 1967), 274–77; David Hecht, *Russian Radicals Look to America, 1825–1894* (Cambridge, Mass., 1947), 1–15.

[38] E. H. Carr, *The Romantic Exiles, A Nineteenth Century Portrait Gallery* (New York, 1975); Alexander Kukcherov, "Alexander Herzen's Parallel Between the United States and Russia," in John Shelton Curtiss, ed., *Essays in Russian and Soviet History in Honor of Gerard Tanquary Robinson* (New York, 1963), 34–47.

ing Siberian exile by way of America, Bakunin spent a few months there and gained many of his impressions from the visit. He attributed America's fortunate "exceptionalism" to abundant land and thought it temporary, but he retained his belief in America's future. The available alternatives that remained were "America or eastern barbarism." Of all this generation of Russian radicals, Nicholas Chernyshevski was the most voluble, unqualified, and lavish in his praise, though he limited it strictly to the northern free states. He overdid his praise of the North and exaggerated its difference from the South, which he equated with the difference between Switzerland and Naples. Slavery was the only blot on the American scene for him. Apart from that, or once it was removed, he seemed virtually blind to the numerous faults and injustices that marred the American scene. Long imprisoned or in Siberian exile, he never visited the country himself. [39]

The first serious, comprehensive report on America by a Russian observer was a book in two volumes by Aleksandr Borisovich Lakier, the fruit of an extensive tour of settled parts of the country he made in 1857. A rather obscure figure otherwise, Lakier never published anything else and was soon forgotten. But the book on his American travels has provoked comparison with that of Tocqueville, not for its depth or fame but for its similarities of purpose. "What could we derive for our own benefit and edification," he asked, "from the great experience represented by America," and what was "the core of that democratic equality which is quite incomprehensible to a European?" These were certainly Tocquevillean questions, but Lakier asked them with more eagerness, hopefulness, and optimism than did the melancholy young Frenchman. Whether it was prisons, jury trial, police, fire-fighters, public schools, or railroad construction, the American way was implicitly seen and pictured as a model for emulation or a criticism of the Russian way. His few attacks on American

[39] Hecht, *Russian Radicals*, 48–141.

institutions were similarly used: criticism of slavery strongly implied criticism of Russian serfdom without mentioning the serf. Lakier confidently predicted the peaceful spread of American influence in Europe, and declared that "this influence will be more durable than any conquest."[40]

The long period of relative harmony and cordiality in relations between Russia and America in foreign policy reached a high point in the purchase of Alaska. The next half-century, from 1867 to 1917, was marked by gradual deterioration and conflicting interests between the two countries. The course of international relations was shaped by national self-interest and reasons of state that did not necessarily determine intellectual attitudes and popular sympathies. Whether by coincidence or otherwise, however, a simultaneous shift away from the long-prevailing intellectual and radical sympathies for America could be observed in some quarters.

One illustration of the change comes from the inner circle of radicals, noted for the most part for their pro-American leanings. The deviant was Peter Lavrov, prominent socialist writer living in forced exile, who voiced his views on America mainly in the 1870s. While he retained from his earlier attachment some ambiguities about American institutions, his disillusionment after the Civil War and his disgust with postwar venality and deteriorating standards was virtually complete—and largely justified. His rhetoric about "that model product of political liberalism" became at times a tirade against "the republic of humbug."[41]

Among the contemporary generation of great Russian novelists, Fydor Dostoyevsky cast aside an early fondness for America. In four of his last five novels, those written between 1866 and 1881, he made reference to America as a means of escape, but always negatively—sometimes as an alternative to suicide. In *Crime and Punishment* suicide wins, the victim's

[40] Arnold Schrier and Joyce Story, tr. and ed., *A Russian Looks at America, The Journey of Aleksandr Borisovich Lakier in 1857* (Chicago and London, 1979), 5–6, 47–48, 52–53, 57, 86–87, 212–19, 261.
[41] Hecht, *Russian Radicals*, 152, 162, 167, 194, 219.

last words before pulling the trigger being, "If you are asked, say I said I was off to America." And in *The Brothers Karamazov*, Mitya pronounces America "as bad, perhaps, as Siberia. . . . I hate that America already . . . they are not of my soul. I love Russia. . . . I shall choke there!"[42] On the other hand, Ivan Turgenev claimed to have earned the nickname "the American" in his student days because of his enthusiasm for the republic, an attitude he never entirely abandoned. Count Tolstoy, like Turgenev, never came to America, but he expressed a special attachment for it, continued to read everything he could about it, and to receive visits from American admirers. In 1890 he wrote of it as the land "to which I feel most powerfully bound."[43]

A break in the long tradition of Russian men of letters was most sharply marked by Maxim Gorky in what he wrote about his visit to New York in 1906. His avowed purpose by this time was to use his writing as a revolutionary tool and particularly to discredit the old image of a democratic American society cherished by liberals and radicals. In place of the traditional image he pictured a New World society that was a nightmare of poverty, dullness, misery, and squalor. New York was "a monstrous city," a "cramped prison for everyone," its people "enslaved" and it was "terrible and painful" to speak of them. His own feelings were another matter. At the same time he was writing this he was telling his friends in letters to Russia how "amazingly interesting" and "devilishly beautiful" a land it was, "a marvelous country for a man who can work and wants to work," he declared. "What they accomplish, these devils, how they work . . . it's both sickening and enjoyable, and— it's a hell of a lot of fun!"[44]

The same ambiguous doublethink about America con-

---

[42] *Crime and Punishment*, 2nd ed., tr. J. Coulson, ed. George Gibian (New York, 1978), 433; *The Brothers Karamazov*, tr. Constance Garnett (New York, 1950), 926.

[43] Dieter Boden, *Das Amerikabild im russichen Schriften bis zum Ende des 19. Jahrhunderts* (Hamburg, 1968), 167–73.

[44] *America Through Russian Eyes, 1874–1926*, ed. and tr. Olga Peters Harty and Susanne Fusso (New Haven, 1988), 128–40.

tinued before 1917 even among communist revolutionaries and with it a great deal of the old will to believe and see or hope for the miracles of progress in the land of western energy. This mood did not end abruptly with the October Revolution. Official Soviet policy, of course, placed the United States among the hostile capitalist powers who were by nature enemies of the cause of revolution and ruthless exploiters of labor everywhere. Nevertheless the government continued to tolerate, even foster the conception of the United States as a technological model for the Soviet Union and thought of modernization as synonymous with Americanization, however abhorrent politically and socially it might be.

One colorful example of this mixture of attitudes was the young poet Vladimir Mayakovsky, who visited America for a few months in 1925 and hastily published "My Discovery of America'.' after he returned home. An enthusiastic supporter of the revolution, he nevertheless had difficulty tempering his unqualified delight with technology in "the land where the 'future,' at least in terms of industrialization, is being realized." He put in suitable negative commentary about labor unrest at living conditions, but his raptures and awe over technological wonders burst into lyrical expression. Brooklyn Bridge inspired a long poem. Even the efficiency of Chicago slaughterhouses impressed him. He concluded with the assurance that the "goal of my sketches is to force people to study the weak and strong sides of America in anticipation of the battle ahead in the distant future." Russian critics, with some justification, pronounced the book superficial.[45]

The Great Depression of the 1930s, which produced such bitterness among nations, curiously enough provided the background for much Russian good will and admiration for Americans. Hundreds of American engineers played a role in

[45] Edward J. Brown, Mayakovsky, a Poet in the Revolution (Princeton, 1973), 191–97; Charles Rougle, Three Russians Consider America: America in the Works of Maksim Gor'kij, Alexandr Blok, and Vladimir Mayakovskij (Stockholm, 1976), 97–146.

high pressure Soviet industrialization, and American workmen and tourists came by the thousands. As one of the tourists
in the summer of 1932, I personally and repeatedly experi-
enced the friendly mood of ordinary Russian people toward
Americans. Implicit in the Soviet program of "overtaking and
surpassing" America industrially was an acknowledgment of
America as a model for Soviet emulation. "We have learned a
lot already and have still to learn a few things from Americans," said Minister of Food Mikoyan on returning from the
United States in 1936 and importing typical American food
products and a fast-food automat for Moscow.[46]

In the same year two respected and admired Soviet
satirists, Ilya Ilf and Eugene Petrov, returned from a tour of
America and in 1937 published a book entitled in English
translation *Little Golden America*. Famous in its time but
largely forgotten now, it evidently told Soviet readers what
they wanted to hear about America. Greeted by John dos
Passos and Ernest Hemingway when they arrived in New
York, the authors were advised on their cross-country itiner-
ary, and took off in a newly purchased Ford with an American
driver. Much of their adventure reads like pure tourism: "The
Empire State Building, Niagara, the Ford plant, the Grand
Canyon, Boulder Dam, sequoias, and now the suspension
bridges of San Francisco." The scene that unrolls along the
superhighways is a technological wonderland and a con-
sumers' paradise of Soviet dreams with all the supermarkets
and fast food they aspired to and still lacked. All this, it should
be remembered, unfolds in an America of breadlines, unemployment, and dust bowls, the time of *The Grapes of Wrath*,
when the Depression was approaching bottom. In fairness to
Ilya and Petrov, they are quite aware of the American paradox
of plenty and poverty, unemployment, and misery all around
them. It would seem an ideal opportunity to make Marxist

---

[46] Frederick C. Barghoorn, *The Soviet Image of the United States, A Study in Distortion* (New York, 1950), 21–35.

propaganda. They do supply a few dutiful stereotypes, but content themselves largely, in a chapter called "They and We," with reflections on their beloved homeland. "And throughout that entire journey we never once stopped thinking of the Soviet Union." They conclude (whether with tongue in cheek or not), that communist people "by comparison with Americans of the average kind, are now already much calmer and happier than they." That was because they pursued the goal set by Stalin, "To catch up with America!" in a communal and not a competitive way. The book does not seem to have been received as an unfriendly one.[47]

Hard upon this era followed two terrible wars: one in which the two great countries were allies, the Second World War; then another in which they were opponents, the long Cold War. Whether as allies or as opponents, whether in shooting wars or in wars of another kind, participants normally employ written words as weapons—not for purposes that have engaged our interest in these pages. A welcome return to written discourse of the latter sort under the dispensation of *glasnost* promised for a while material for a new and happier chapter on the old Russo-American counterpoint.

[47] Ilya Ilf and Eugene Petrov, *Little Golden America*, tr. Charles Malamuth (London, 1944), 287–92.

6

Tantalus Americanus

EQUALITY WAS THE AMERICAN HERESY most widely advertised abroad, and when foreigners came to America or read about it, they sought evidence to confirm their expectations. Some found such evidence even before the heresy received its classic formulation in Thomas Jefferson's preamble to the Declaration. Few of them were interested in the fine points that American theorists made about equality, such as equality between Englishmen in the colonies and Englishmen at home, or equality of Americans before the law.[1] The sort of equality Europeans expected and sought to find in the New World was equality of status, equality between bottom and top of the social order, the reverse of the Old World hierarchical society of fixed and unequal "estates."

Europeans usually found what they were looking for in the New World, some to their gratified horror, some to their eager delight. The search had varied purposes. The seekers often found more equality than was actually there, for there was ample evidence of inequality overlooked. They overlooked what to them was not remarkable and singled out what

[1] J. R. Pole, *The Pursuit of Equality in American History* (Berkeley, 1978), 24–37.

was. What was remarkable, among other things, was the contrast between the condition and attitudes among the lower class at home and in America. All of their impressions were comparative, and that was their standard of comparison: class relations in Europe. It was what the Marquis de Chastellux had in mind in 1783 when he remarked on the wages of American workers producing such "a state of equality that the same enjoyments which would be deemed superfluous in every other part of the world are here considered as necessities."[2] The same comparison inspired a second French aristocrat in the next decade to wonder at tea and coffee and meat twice a day being regular fare "in the most miserable hut," and "the proverbial wish of *having* a chicken in the pot" being a *fait accompli.*[3] "What a contrast between Europe and America!" wrote the socialist Michel Chevalier in 1838. "After landing in New York, I thought every day was Sunday," because the throngs on Broadway dressed that way in this "land of promise for the labouring class."[4] To Francis Grund it seemed that American mechanics enjoyed "comforts which would hardly enter the imagination of similar orders in Europe."[5] "Happy is the country," wrote Harriet Martineau, "where the factory-girls carry parasols, and pig-drivers wear spectacles."[6]

In the very opening sentence of the first volume of his *Democracy in America*, Alexis de Tocqueville sounded this note as his basic theme. "Among the novel objects that attracted my attention during my stay in the United States," he

[2] Chastellux to the Rev. James Madison, Jan. 12, 1783, in François-Jean Marquis de Chastellux, *Travels in North America, in the Years 1780, 1781, and 1782* . . . (2 vols., London, 1787), II, 535.

[3] François Alexander Frédéric, duc de La Rochefoucauld-Liancourt, *Travels Through the United States of North America* . . . (2 vols., London 1799), II, 672.

[4] Michel Chevalier, *Society, Manners and Politics in the United States: Being a Series of Letters on North America* (Boston, 1839), 341–42.

[5] Francis J. Grund, *The Americans in Their Moral, Social, and Political Relations* (Boston, 1837), 290.

[6] Quoted in Frederick Marryat, *A Diary in America*, ed. Sydney Jackman (New York, 1962), 229.

wrote, "nothing struck me more forcibly than the general equality of conditions among the people. . . . it creates opinions, gives birth to new sentiments, founds novel customs, and modifies whatever it does not produce." He went further. "The more I advanced in the study of American society, the more I perceived that this equality of condition is the fundamental fact from which all others seem to be derived, and the central point at which all my observations constantly terminated."[7]

The "equality of condition" that so beguiled Tocqueville and his contemporaries in the 1830s became less visible among working classes and the lower orders, particularly of urban society, in the following decade of depression. One of the few foreign celebrities to step away from the brilliant throngs of Broadway for a look at what lay beyond was Charles Dickens. In 1842 he did not have to go more than a block to find himself in the midst of the vilest and most notorious slum in the country. Accompanied by policemen he climbed the stairs of tenements and explored alleys, "narrow ways, diverging to right and left, and reeking everywhere with dirt and filth." He described human misery, poverty, and disease that made mockery of the pretensions of equality.[8] Nor was degradation confined to city slums. Out in the back country of Illinois where life was said to begin anew another traveler found settlers living like "pigs in the woods" in a condition of barbarism, "with nothing like satisfaction or happiness."[9] Another found the lower class of the backwoods "the most abject that, perhaps, ever peopled a Christian land," living in log hovels "more wretched than can be conceived," worse than "the huts of the poor of Ireland."[10]

[7] Alexis de Tocqueville, *Democracy in America* (2 vols., New York, 1972), I, 3.

[8] Charles Dickens, *American Notes* (Gloucester, Mass., 1968), 108–19.

[9] William Faux, *Memorable Days in America: Being a Journal of a Tour to the United States . . . Intended to Show Men and Things As They Are in America* (London, 1823), 125–27.

[10] Charles William Janson, *The Stranger in America, 1793–1806* (reprinted from the London edition of 1807; New York, 1935), 88, 304, 310–11.

The aspect of the American paradox of equality that puzzled foreigners even more was the persistence and growth of the egalitarian presumptions among the lower classes. Even the backwoods wretches described as the most abject in Christendom were found to "consider themselves on an equal footing with the best educated people of the country, and upon the principle of equality they intrude themselves into every company." The most objectionable aspect of equality was the confusion of ranks. The "arrogance of domestics" was "particularly calculated to excite the astonishment of strangers." One could not tell from their manner or even their clothes whether they were menials. Policemen, firemen, and train conductors did not then usually wear uniforms. No whites would answer to the name of "servant" or admit to having a "master." They insisted on being called the "help."[11]

The genuine aristocrat was likely to take all this more casually, in the spirit of a visiting amateur anthropologist. The Duke de La Rochefoucauld-Liancourt, for example, was amused in the late eighteenth century to have the driver of the stagecoach join him at the dinner table, but reflected that "it would seem equally strange to Americans to see the coachman eating by himself." In fact, "the circumstance of our servants not dining with us at the same table," he observed, "excited general astonishment." The duke accommodated himself philosophically at several inns to the waiters seating themselves with him at meals after serving him, and the landlord attending his guest's wants with his hat on his head.[12] Europeans of middling ranks were less likely to accept such conduct with detachment. Fanny Kemble pronounced her American inferiors "never servile, and but seldom civil," though she rather liked their independence of mind. Frances Trollope condidered all this talk of equality "a spur to that coarse familiarity, untampered by any shadow of respect, which is

11 Ibid., 310–11.
12 La Rochefoucauld-Liancourt, Travels, I, 23–24, 68.

assumed by the grossest and the lowest in their intercourse with the highest and most refined."[13] Gustaf Unonius noted how quickly newly arrived immigrants shifted from "being too humble and subservient" to conduct calculated to prove "that they knew their rights and that in America one man is as good as another. "Many a time," he said, "it happened that I found it difficult to make an immigrant keep his hat on his head when he was talking with me in the street, and a few days later I had still more trouble to persuade him to remove it when he came to call on me in my house." The title "gentleman" was "given indiscriminately to any man," and "lady" was "a synonym for woman," but more particularly for subordinates, as in "cleaning lady," a term still quite common to the present day.[14]

Karl Baedeker's guide book for tourists in the United States attests the durability of these customs. Under a section of the book entitled "General Hints," Baedeker advised that one "accommodate oneself to the customs of the country." More specifically the tourist "should from the outset reconcile himself to the absence of deference or servility on the part of those he considers his social inferiors." This advice continued to appear in every edition of Baedeker's guide from the first in 1893 to the one of 1909.[15] A tourist in 1904 called it a good piece of advice and observed that foreigners who failed to take it would "probably live in a perpetual state of indignation and annoyance."[16]

Europeans could not agree among themselves about the affect of equality upon manners. Predominantly they tended to associate equality with the lowering of standards and blame it for the vulgarity and crassness they abhorred. Thus Mrs.

[13] Frances A. Kemble, *Journal of a Residence in America* (Paris, 1835), 182n. Frances Trollope, *Domestic Manners of the Americans*, ed. Donald Smalley (New York, 1949), 121.

[14] *The Memoirs of Gustaf Unonius, A Pioneer in Northwest America, 1841–1856* (2 vols., Minneapolis, 1960), II, 109–11, 116–17, 139.

[15] Karl Baedeker, *The United States with Excursions to Mexico, Cuba, Porto Rico, and Alaska* . . . (New York and London, 1909), xxvii–xxviii.

[16] Philip Burne-Jones, *Dollars and Democracy* (New York, 1904), 69.

Trollope said that "if refinement once creeps in among them, if they once learn . . . the graces, the honours, the chivalry of life, then we shall say farewell to American equality."[17] Yet Captain Marryat, who cared no more for equality than Mrs. Trollope, thought that civility was "one of the few virtues springing from democracy," if for no other reason than the control of temper imposed by having to treat inferiors as if they were equals.[18] Granting the low state of manners in earlier days, James Bryce maintained that, "Equality improves manners, for it strengthens the basis of all good manners, respect for other men and women simply as men and women, irrespective of their station in life."[19] Even in her day, Harriet Martineau remarked that "the English insolence of class to class, of individuals towards each other is not even conceived of [in America], except in the one highly disgraceful instance of the people of colour," and "the same contempt is spread over the whole society here [in England], which is there concentrated upon the blacks."[20] By the time Beatrice Webb arrived in 1898, it seemed to her that, "Of all the white races the Americans have to-day the most agreeable manners: they are most adept in social amenities. . . . an absence of all, we English call snobbishness."[21] And in the same year James Muirhead singled out "this feeling of equality in the air as a potent enhancer of the pleasures of society," rather than the reverse.[22]

Europeans were as fascinated by the upper ranks and their adjustment to the rule of equality as they were by the lower orders and their conduct. They brought to the one the

[17] F. Trollope, *Domestic Manners of the Americans*, 409.
[18] Marryat, *A Diary in America*, 460–61.
[19] James Bryce, *American Commonwealth* (London, 1888), II, 662.
[20] Harriet Martineau, *Society in America* (New York, 1966), III, 27–28.
[21] Beatrice Webb, *American Diary*, ed. David Shannon (Madison, 1963), 142–43.
[22] James Fullerton Muirhead, *America the Land of Contrasts* (London, 1898), 36.

same standard of comparison they brought to the other—how things were done in the Old World. The contrasts were no less marked, and they were most conspicuous among public officials, starting at the very top. Nothing was simpler than access to the White House through most of the nineteenth century, and a presentation to the President was easy to arrange and startlingly informal. No guards at the gate, no sentries at the door, no police, no soldiers, no servants in livery, and the public rooms "as open to everybody as the reading rooms of a public library," according to a visitor in 1883.[23] From the time of President Monroe to that of McKinley, White House receptions were crowded with citizens of varied ranks mixed with the highest federal officials, civil and military, along with ambassadors of the diplomatic corps. The last were conspicuous for clinging to the splendors of uniform, regalia, and decorations. The contrast they offered at the second inauguration of President McKinley in 1901 is described by one witness: a brilliant array of court uniforms, "Siam, Korea, Hungary, and Portugal as gay as butterflies," against the sober American officials in broadcloth, "without a star, a ribbon, or a sword between them; the effect was almost comic."[24]

Foreigners encountered the same rule of accessibility, informality, and absence of ceremony up and down the ranks of officialdom, including cabinet ministers, generals, bishops, governors. A Norwegian was startled to be presented to the governor of a western state and recognize him as a man he had seen half an hour before in work clothes repairing his chimney.[25] On enquiring for the governor of Arkansas at his home, another foreigner was informed by the first lady of that state that his Excellency "was gone to the woods to hunt for a sow

[23] W. E. Adams, *Our American Cousins: Being Personal Impressions of the People and Institutions of the United States* (London, 1883), 107.

[24] Frederic Harrison, *Memories and Thoughts* (New York, 1906), 189.

[25] Ole Munch Raeder, *America in the Forties* (Minneapolis, 1929), 81–82.

and pigs belonging to her. . . ."[26] Such experiences con-
firmed the opinion of foreign critics of the democracy that
public office was not to be had without abandonment of
dignity and that as a consequence the occupant of such office
was deprived of authority and respect.

In private life, on the other hand, the wealthy citizen was
seen as salvaging much authority and respect as well as
privilege by leading what might be described as a double life.
In public he avoided display and walked humbly with his
inferiors, but in private he led a very different life. "His dress is
plain," as Tocqueville described him, "his demeanor un-
assuming; but the interior of his dwelling glitters with luxury,
and none but a few chosen guests, whom he haughtily styled
his equals, are allowed to penetrate into this sanctuary. No
European noble is more jealous of the smallest advantages that
a privileged station confers."[27]

The advantages of privilege and wealth continued to be
noted by foreign observers, but after Tocqueville less and less
was heard from them about the concealment of wealth and
public humility of the wealthy. Instead they spoke more and
more about the open display and flaunting of wealth, of crass
extravagance and public luxury, of haughty and snobbish
behavior. European critics were especially hard on the pretensions of the northern aristocracy of the 1840s and 1850s. They
saw clearly enough that it was based on wealth, and for the
most part on very new wealth at that. Lacking any foundation
of birth, title, or tradition, and any significant support from
the old colonial elite, they were perceived as a pretentious
nouveaux riches. "There can be nothing more absurd,"
declared an aristocrat of Irish origins, "than to hear the
wealthy classes in North American cities boast of their 'fashionable society' and their 'aristocracy,' and make announce-

[26]G. W. Featherstonehough, *Excursion Through the Slave States* (2 vols.,
London, 1844), II, 53.
[27]Tocqueville, *Democracy in America*, I, 180.

ments of events in 'high life.'" In his opinion "it takes three generations to make a gentleman" and in America "such a thing as grandfather, father, and son in one family preserving their fortune and station is almost unheard of."[28]

Yet a German nobleman said he had "heard more talk about aristocracy and family in the United States than during my whole previous life in Europe." It was an obsession with them. "In point of accomplishment they are inferior to the middle classes of Europe; but in pride and conceit they surpass the ancient nobility of the Holy Roman Empire and the thirty-four princes of the actual Germanic Confederation."[29] In the 1850s private coaches with heraldric crests and coachmen and footmen in livery were to be seen in the streets of New York. Europeans described Americans abroad as tuft-hunters and toadies among aristocratic circles. At home fashionable social climbers competed in doing homage with lavish entertainment to visiting princes, dukes, and barons.[30] The marriage market for American heiresses seeking foreign titles was thriving well before the Civil War.

The surest and most dependable means for an aristocracy of wealth to compete in the establishment of status lay in conspicuous display. The confinement of display to domestic interiors that had impressed Tocqueville very quickly went public. Europeans marveled at the evidence of this in the land of equality, at the brand-new palatial mansions, the wild extravagance of dress, the expensive jewelry, and the prodigiously expensive parties. William Makepeace Thackeray during his American tour in 1852 wrote, "I never saw such luxury and extravagance, such tearing polkas, such stupendous suppers and fine clothes."[31] It was hard to match in

[28]Thomas Holley Grattan, *Civilized America* (2 vols., London 1859), I, 117–18, 189.
[29]Quoted by Francis J. Grund, *Aristocracy in America* (New York, 1959; original ed., 1839), 145, 301.
[30]Ibid., 302.
[31]Quoted in Douglas T. Miller, *Jacksonian Aristocracy, Class and Democracy in New York, 1830–1860* (New York, 1967), 163.

Europe at a period known for extravagant living. It was scarcely exceeded in lavishness and vulgarity by the later period of American history known as the Gilded Age. That period in many respects simply continued, extended, and elaborated the characteristics of the earlier one.

The serpent of exclusiveness in the garden of equality troubled and puzzled European observers, and few failed to note its presence in society as distinct from government. After three extended visits in the 1870s and 1880s, Emily Faithfull, the English feminist, concluded that "all candid persons will acknowledge to a growing love of caste distinctions in that country. Society there has its dividing lines, its high fences, which separate individuals dwelling in the same city, as distinctly as prejudice, blood, or education . . . in the Old World."[32] One theory they advanced to explain the anomaly was that the very absence of tradition, rank, and title that established social gradations in the Old World made exclusiveness more arbitrary, harsh, and self-conscious in the New. Another theory had it that since equality of opportunity excluded almost no white man from competition, the competition was all the more fierce, open, and defensive.[33] "Competition,—that is the secret of the American system," avowed the Americanized Frenchman Achille Murat; "every thing is to be won by competition; fortune, power, love, riches, all these objects of desire are attainable; it is for the most skillful to go in pursuit of them."[34] Among legitimate objects of competitive pursuit were social status and exclusiveness.

Among those who were the chief beneficiaries of this competition, the upper class and especially the rich, Tocqueville noted "a hearty dislike of the democratic institutions of

---

[32] Emily Faithfull, *Three Visits to America* (New York, 1884), 35–36.

[33] Adam G. Gurowski, *America and Europe* (New York, 1857), 402, 408; Edward Sullivan, *Rambles and Scrambles in North and South America* (London, 1853), 182.

[34] Achille Murat, *A Moral and Political Sketch of the United States of America* (London, 1833), 343.

their country" and a strong class bias against the masses who "form a power which they at once fear and despise." Francis Grund called it "absolute contempt, and sometimes hatred of the institutions," which such people consider "opposed to national grandeur" as well as to their class interests. They were capable of "rudeness, insolence, and effrontery" toward their inferiors. He was told that "Prince Metternich cannot hold the Radicals in greater abhorrence than they are held by the wealthy merchants, lawyers, and bankers in the United States," and that "Robespierre is not more detested in France, than Jefferson and Jackson are among the higher classes in America."[35] Fanny Kemble was one among several who noted "how singular the contrast was between the levelling spirit of this government, and the separating and dividing spirit of American society." It was an anomaly, she thought, that "democracy governs the land; whilst, through society, a contrary tendency shows itself, wherever it can obtain the smallest opportunity."[36] Whether the tendency of government or that of society would prevail in the end was a matter of dispute.

The fault most commonly agreed upon by European critics of democratic government in the United States was its failure to attract men of talent and distinction to public life and political office. This criticism was common among friendly and unfriendly critics from Tocqueville to Bryce and on into the twentieth century. They agreed that in its launching and early years the republic did indeed attract men of talent, and they agreed that it soon ceased to do so, but they were at odds on the reasons for these developments. In some of his harshest judgments, Tocqueville flatly attributes the low character of American political leadership "to the ever increasing despotism of the majority in the United States," and suggests that to bow to its will one must "almost abjure one's qualities as a

---

[35] Tocqueville, *Democracy in America*, I, 180; Grund, *Aristocracy in America*, 85, 112, 174.

[36] Kemble, *Journal of a Residence in America*, 137n.

man," acquire "the temper of a lackey," and undergo "debasement of character."[37] Critics with more conservative leanings and a few with less took up and repeated this theme, often elaborating on the degrading consequences. According to one, all men of probity "turn from the scene of politics with horror and disgust"; to another it was plain that "the scum is uppermost," and that "the prudent, the enlightened, the wise, and the good have all retired into the shade" rather than abandon honor, pride, and dignity and court favor with the mob.[38] The result was described by a third as a "wild, democratic, mannerless, and tyrannical rule" attributed to "the fatal substitution of universal suffrage for character and property."[39] Political life in the mid-1880s was still said to be "shunned by an honest man as the plague."[40]

For all his good will, James Bryce in his time could still not deny the persistent failure of American political life to attract recruits from the higher social ranks and greatest ability. He did not, however, think democracy was the reason for this and rejected the whole traditional line of reasoning. Instead he offered a complex explanation and many reasons, most of which followed from what appeared to him the unchallengeable assumption that, "Politics are less interesting than in Europe." By that he meant the absence in America of the deep conflicts over foreign policy, constitutional change, class privilege, religious freedom, and what he described as "an upward pressure of the poorer or the unprivileged masses." To him there seemed to be left in America "no class privileges or religious inequalities to be abolished."[41]

Bryce was anticipated a generation before by a fellow Scotsman, Alexander Mackay, who undertook to explain the comparative pettiness of American politics. Granting that in

[37] Tocqueville, Democracy in America, I, 266–67.
[38] Thomas Brothers, The United States of North America As They Are; Not As They Are Generally Described: Being a Cure for Radicalism (London, 1840), 147–48; Marryat, A Diary in America, 438–39.
[39] Featherstonehough, Excursion Through the Slave States, I, xxiv–xxv.
[40] Lepel Griffin, The Great Republic (London, 1884), 1–2.
[41] Bryce, American Commonwealth, II, 37–43.

European politics "great principles" and "mighty moral forces" inspired enthusiasm that was "terrible, dangerous, whilst it is sublime," he contrasted that with "the stereotyped zeal of the American politician and the petty objects on which it is expended." But the contrast was accounted for in his belief that, "The grand principles for which the people elsewhere are still fighting, and which give to political warfare its more dignified and imposing forms, have all been conceded" in America. [42] That was to overlook one of the things that had not at that time been conceded—the freedom of millions of black slaves in America. The resolution of that issue was to outdo anything Europe had to offer in the nineteenth century in the way of "grand principles" and "mighty moral forces," sublime and otherwise.

Of all the paradoxes and ironies in American equality, those presented by slavery and race intrigued Europeans the most. The critics from the time of Dr. Samuel Johnson, with his quip about "the loudest *yelps* for liberty among the drivers of negroes," had their laughs and taunts; while admirers and well-wishers had their embarrassments and disenchantments. All had their say. Even the revolutionary pro-Americans in the time of the Mirage had to acknowledge the facts, even a Brissot, a Chastellux, and a Crèvecœur. The Polish patriot Niemcewicz, who all but worshiped General Washington, looked into his hero's slave huts and pronounced them "more miserable than the most miserable of the cottages of our peasants."[43] No radical could match the Hungarian Alexander Farkas in adulation and praise of American institutions; yet he could write, "I felt as if an icy hand had touched my heart," as soon as he entered a slave state. [44] With the best will for sympathetic understanding, Michel Chevalier was re-

[42] Alexander Mackay, *The Western World; or, Travels in the United States in 1846–47* . . . (2 vols., Philadelphia, 1849), I, 213–14.

[43] Julian Ursyn Niemcewicz, *Under Their Vine and Fig Tree. Travels Through America in 1797–1799, 1805 with Some Further Account of Life in New Jersey* (Elizabeth, N.J., 1965), 100.

[44] Alexander Farkas, *Journey in North America* (Philadelphia, 1977), 168.

volted by what he saw in Virginia,[45] and so were other Europeans who came with good will and the best intentions. An Oxford don discovered that what he had assumed to be a "libel had become a criminal indictment; . . . the former plaintiff was the defendant," and the don was "now in the witness-box."[46]

Much of the testimony, especially that of professed abolitionists, was of a familiar type, with descriptions of the auction block, divided families, and slave coffles on the march. At the height of anti-slavery agitation, the South came to be regarded as a sort of American Siberia, and few Europeans ventured below the Potomac very far. Those who did, including some with an avowed distaste for slavery, regularly confessed a decided preference for the company of southern whites of the upper class over that of the northerners of the same class. Southerners were said to "resemble Europeans" more than Yankees in their manners, conversation, philosophy, and style of life.[47] Tocqueville found them "more clever, more frank, more generous, more intellectual, and more brilliant," and thought they had both the strengths and weaknesses "of all aristocracies," while northerners combined "good and bad qualities of the middle classes."[48] James Buckingham, British member of Parliament, contrasted the grace, dignity, kindness and suavity of the South with "the coldness, formality, and reserve of the North."[49]

No European has been discovered in the act of deliberately attempting to reconcile American slavery with American

[45] Chevalier, Society, Manners and Politics, 327.
[46] E. S. Abdy, Journal of a Residence and Tour in the United States of North America, From April, 1833 to October, 1834 (3 vols., London, 1833), I, 391–92.
[47] Kemble, Journal of a Residence in America, 137n.; also see Chevalier, Society, Manners and Politics, 114–15; Francis Grund, The Americans in Their Moral, Social, and Political Relations (Boston, 1837), 374; Thomas Hamilton, Men and Manners in America (2 vols., Philadelphia, 1833), II, 145; Mackay, The Western World, I, 131–33, 255–57; Fredrica Bremer, Homes in the New World (New York, 1853), I, 383.
[48] Tocqueville, Democracy in America, I, 395.
[49] James Silk Buckingham, The Slave States of America (2 vols., London, 1842), I, 122.

professions of equality. There were, however, occasional flashes of insight suggesting a deeper vein of irony and paradox connecting American slavery and American equality than the one Dr. Johnson had in mind. It was ironic, of course, that the "the loudest *yelps* for liberty" came from slave owners during the Revolution. But Sir Augustus John Foster, Secretary of the British Legation during Jefferson's administration, had a different irony in mind when he observed that, "Owners of slaves, among themselves, are all for keeping down every kind of superiority." They were able to "profess an unbounded love of liberty and of democracy in consequence of the mass of people, who in other countries might become mobs, being nearly altogether composed of their own Negro slaves."[50] When all who were white were invited to join the brotherhood of the free and equal and look down upon all who were black, unfree, and unequal, then American slavery did take on an ironic reconciliation with American equality—as its underpinning, the underpinning of a strictly white egalitarianism.

Mrs. Trollope detested the airs, pretensions, and what she contemptuously called "the fallacious ideas of equality, which are so fondly cherished by the working classes of the white population in America." She thought these working-class delusions were "in fact generated solely by the existence of slavery" and that once it was abolished "the gradation of ranks INEVITABLE in the progress of society would take place naturally"—that is, the working class would behave with what she considered proper subordination and humility.[51] Trying to explain why "a working man in this country is situated very differently from one of his class at home," a Scottish worker in America also pointed to slavery. "The relationship which exists between slaves and their owners in this land of liberty,"

[50] Augustus John Foster, Bart., *Jeffersonian America. Notes on the United States of America Collected in the Years 1805–6–7 and 11–12*, ed. Richard Beale Davis (San Marino, Calif., 1954).
[51] F. Trollope, *Domestic Manners of the Americans*, 186 and fn.

he wrote in 1865, "has been the means of kicking the word 'master' from the Yankee vocabulary, and the quaint phrase of 'Boss' has been substituted in its place." Under these conditions, "Jack is as good as his master," and with most of the menial and degrading work done by slaves and blacks, the status of white labor, "instead of being a thing of reproach, as in the old world, confers a dignity upon its professors."[52] Emancipation did not change the color or drastically alter the status of the freedmen, and black labor of degraded status continued long after the end of slavery to provide an underpinning and support for the way of life and posture of equality among white labor. After slavery was abolished, however, its black victims faded rapidly from European attention.

American women, from the start, never lacked European attention. They were, in fact, a peculiar subject of interest, the subject of at least a chapter and often more in almost every European book on America through the nineteenth and twentieth centuries. Commenting on this special interest and pointing out that there was no corresponding attention to women in books about other countries, James F. Muirhead, British compiler of Baedeker's guide, explained: "The European visitor to the United States *has* to write about American women because they bulk so largely in his view, because .. . their relative importance and interest impress him as greater than those of women in the lands of the Old World, because they seem to him to embody in so eminent a measure that intangible quality of Americanism."[53] That intangible quality took many forms, but prominent among them were the ways in which women attained or failed to attain the American promise of equality.

Nineteenth-century Europeans could almost be said to have been persuaded to a man—though hardly to a woman—

[52] James Dawson Burn, *Three Years Among the Working-Classes in the United States. During the War* (London, 1865), 42, 72.
[53] Muirhead, *America the Land of Contrasts*, 46.

that American women enjoyed a higher status than did the women of the Old World. Their commonest observation, with virtually no dissent, was the extraordinary deference that men paid women, at least in all public and observable circumstances. This was not equality but privilege, a kind of reverse discrimination. It was variously described as "quixotic devotion," as a "quaint gallantry," sometimes as "idolatry," or simply as kindness, consideration, or respect. It amounted to a rigid code of public etiquette. At a minimum it permitted women unusual freedom of movement, for they were said to travel any distance alone with complete security and no fear of harassment. The code also often accorded them offer of the best seat, the best view, the first place in line. Foreigners complained that women accepted these favors as their right without the slightest sign of acknowledgment.[54]

The privileged treatment, however, came at a cost, and the cost was a pedestaled isolation, a rather empty privilege at best. In effect, women were subject to a system of segregation in the name of "protection." Public buildings had ladies' doors, ladies' tables, ladies' drawing rooms; boats had ladies' sides, trains ladies' coaches, and postoffices ladies' windows. Even private entertainment sometimes segregated women at dinner and regularly after dinner because, it was explained, "the gentlemen liked it better." The rule was "respectful and icy propriety," and the result was a melancholy lot of wallflowers, especially married ones. It was a common complaint that "at every turn it is necessary to make separate provision for ladies."[55] For all the privilege and gallantry, men were not willing to let women compete with them in the professions, opportunities, or jobs. Some women, including Frances

[54]Francis Lieber, *The Stranger in America* . . . (Philadelphia, 1835), 69–71; Marryat, *A Diary in America*, 166; Richard Cobden, *The American Diaries*, ed. Elizabeth Cawley (Princeton, 1952), 209; Mackay, *The Western World*, I, 139; William Saunders, *Through the Light Continent* . . . (London, 1879), 481.

[55]Captain Basil Hall, *Travels in North America* . . . (2 vols., Philadelphia, 1829), II, 195; A. Trollope, *North America*, I, 407; F. Trollope, *Domestic Manners of the Americans*, 155–56.

Wright surprisingly, were impressed by "deference," but not Harriet Martineau, who scorned "so much boasting of the 'chivalrous' treatment." According to her opinion American men had "in their treatment of women, fallen below, not only their own democratic principles, but the practice of some parts of the Old World. . . . While woman's intellect is confined, her morals crushed, her health ruined, her weaknesses encouraged, and her strength punished, she is told that her lot is cast in the paradise of women."[56]

"Paradise" was, of course, "woman's place," the home. Male Europeans had a great deal to say, on a basis of rather limited observation, about life in American homes and particularly woman's place in them. As a rule they preferred American domestic life, at least the small and upper-class sample of it they saw, to American public and business life, which was often not to their taste. As one of them observed, home life was "fenced round by as many lines as social life in Europe," which meant "equality without—exclusiveness within." The men of the house took care of the rough democracy outside the home, but did not bring it indoors.[57] There women appeared by the 1880s to hold "undisputed sway" to a degree unknown in the earlier years of the century. The melancholy, segregated wallflowers of former days had given way to vigorous women in full command of themselves and their men.[58]

The European tourist, particularly the male of the species around the turn of the century and after, expressed decided preference for American women over the men. European men were given to extravagant estimates of women's freedom, their "emancipation," even their "dominance" in American society. The praise they lavished on the beauty,

[56] Frances Wright, *Views of Society and Manners in America* . . . (New York, 1821), 312–13; Martineau, *Society in America*, I, 200; III, 105–6.

[57] Mackay, *The Western World*, I, 129.

[58] Faithfull, *Three Visits to America*, 343; Bryce, *American Commonwealth*, II, 592–93.

brilliance, intelligence, and culture of the women they encountered strongly suggests infatuation at times. Two Frenchmen went so far as to compare them with the women of their own country to the disadvantage of the latter. The aging Matthew Arnold, for all his complaints about America, paid tribute to "a charm in American women—a charm which you find in almost all of them." Sir Philip Burne-Jones announced that "America is the land for women—they are queens of the situation all round.[59] A German academician went quite overboard: "The American woman is clever and ingenious and witty; she is brilliant and lively and strong, she is charming and beautiful and noble; she is generous and amiable and resolute . . . indeed, what is she not?"[60]

Their appraisals are subject to discount on several scores. The chief of them is the sample of the female population on which they based their generalizations. It was likely to be much smaller and less typical than their sampling of males, which was not only much larger but more representative if for no other reason than that men were more accessible. The women whom upper-class European men were most likely to meet were far from representative, and they were encountered under circumstances most favorable to them and in which the European felt most at home. "Before such women the European," wrote one of them, "must stand in respectful salute; they embody beauty, grace, intellect—and ideals." And what's more, "The women know Europe intimately," whereas the men were less likely to be as cosmopolitan.[61] Women of this new type had more leisure for cultivation of the arts than their hard-working businessmen husbands. In short, they

[59] Paul Bourget, *Outre-Mer* (New York, 1895), 107–9; Paul Blouet, *Jonathan and His Continent* (New York, 1885), 18; Matthew Arnold, *Civilization in the United States* . . . (Freeport, N.Y., 1972), 168; Burne-Jones, *Dollars and Democracy*, 75.

[60] Hugo Münsterberg, *American Traits* (Boston, 1901), 131.

[61] George Thomas Smart, *The Temper of the American People* (Boston, 1912), 185.

were what Europeans would have liked Americans to be—that is, more like Europeans of their own class. All this had more to do with the superiority than with the equality of women. They were, of course, women of a small and special class, a fact that Europeans sometimes forgot when they generalized about the status of women. "American women enjoy more than equality," concluded a German visitor in 1928; "they occupy a position superior to the man."[62]

Skeptical views also appeared among European appraisals of American women, and they were rather likely to come from European women. Granting that they had more freedom of movement and self-assertion, more deference from men, much greater access to divorce and far more resort to it, and more opportunity to compete as equals with men than did contemporary European women, the skeptics worried about the results of all this. Men spoke of the feminization of American culture, the masculinization of women, the blurring and equalizing of sexual differences, the unresponsiveness and frigidity of women, and the submissiveness of men. European women were less impressed with the rights a few American women had gained and more aware of those yet to be gained by the general run of women. Some of them also expressed doubts about how successfully the American woman reconciled the passive and submissive roles associated with the fulfillment of her basic needs as wife and mother with the aggressive, self-assertive, and competitive attitudes necessary to the fulfillment of her drive for equality.[63] The American pursuit of equality in women's rights and sexual relations appeared to raise as many doubts among Europeans as pursuit of equality did in other aspects of national life.

On no aspect of American domestic life was there more general agreement among European critics than on the distinctiveness of American children. They were different

[62] Arthur Feiler, *America Seen Through German Eyes* (New York, 1928), 250; see also Keyserling, *America Set Free*, 378–79.

[63] Odette Keun, *I Think Aloud in America* (London, 1930), 298–300; Simone de Beauvoir, *The Second Sex* (New York, 1953).

from European children. On that the testimony began very early in the history of the republic, continued in ample flow, and varied little with the nationality or class of the witness. La Rochefoucauld remarked on it in the 1790s and our late contemporary Raymond Aron comments dryly in the 1950s, "The Frenchman does not always regard as charming the American child whose parents apparently grant him complete freedom. Frequently he considers him insufferable."[64] A few, such as Francis Lieber, Harriet Martineau, and Fredrika Bremer, were able to find something to admire in the emancipated child, but they were a minority. For the most part the American child was pronounced a brat or worse and continued to suffer the disfavor and disapproval of European observers for many years.

As described by their foreign critics, the American brats intruded at will upon the company of their elders, showed them no respect, interrupted their conversation, and demanded their attention. They were *heard* as well as seen, voiced opinion on all matters, and flouted all efforts at reproval or discipline. They were likely to make foreign visitors, as one of them confessed, "long strenuously to spank these budding citizens of a free republic, and to send them to bed *instanter*." The adjective most often applied to the budding citizens was "precocious," but it was rarely used with complimentary intent. It meant that they did not behave like children did in Europe where, as Gurowski and others pointed out, youth of all social classes "in all feelings, emotions, as well as worldly concerns, remain children longer than they do in America." Some doubted that many children of America really had any proper childhood at all, but were regarded as "potential adults" and were "prematurely aged" from the start.[65]

---

[64] La Rochefoucauld-Liancourt, *Travels*, I, 552–53; Raymond Aron, in Franz M. Joseph, ed., *As Others See Us: The United States in Foreign Eyes* (Princeton, 1959), 64.

[65] Muirhead, *America the Land of Contrasts*, 64–65; Gurowski, *America and Europe*, 382; Grund, *The Americans*, 136–37; Sullivan, *Rambles and Scrambles*,

Casting about for explanations, critics came eventually to the one often chosen to explain American departures—the influence of democracy and equality. The behavior of children like that of servants, menials, and workmen, was only another instance of the deplorable "loss of that subordination in society which is essentially necessarily to render a country agreeable to foreigners." Here was another example, they said, of democracy misapplied, of equality "where nature designed none." Where was dogma carried to more absurd extreme than where "the theory of the equality of man is rampant in the nursery"? The American child was described as "one of the experiments of democracy," and not the happiest one. Even in working-class families, children "imbibe notions of personal independence at an early stage subversive of all home authority."[66]

American parents received some sympathy but more blame and censure than commiseration. Without much patience, European visitors described the apparent permissiveness, ineffectuality, indulgence, and abdication of authority with which American parents confronted with their children. "'Parents, obey your children in all things,' is the new commandment," according to a critic who thought that "from the child's point of view" America might well be called the "Paradise of Children" and that in the long run it would prove a fool's paradise. "But if the children irritated me," admitted aFrench woman, "the parents maddened me. Their attitude can only be described as a capitulation." Parents idealized and flattered their children shamelessly. "And *how* they praise them—fulsomely, inexhaustibly, to their faces. . . ."[67]

157–58; Edward B. Aveling, *An American Journey* (New York, 1887), 17; David Macrae, *The Americans at Home* . . . (2 vols., Edinburgh, 1870), I, 29–30.

[66] Janson, *The Stranger in America*, 304; Faux, *Journal of a Tour to the United States*, 161–62; Münsterberg, *The Americans* (New York, 1904), 28; Muirhead, *America the Land of Contrasts*, 64; Burn, *Three Years Among the Working-Classes*, 86.

[67] Macrae, *The Americans at Home*, I, 30; Keyserling, *America Set Free*, 324–25; Keun, *I Think Aloud in America*, 306–7.

It was sometimes more than Europeans thought they could endure. And yet there were other times when they were caught off guard and bemused and charmed by some of the results of this misapplied equality. There is the chance experience of Arnold Bennett suddenly encountering a crowd of high-school students. "I had never seen anything like it," he wrote, "that superb stride and carriage in the street. . . . A child is no fool . . . when it sees itself the center of a magnificent pageant, ritual, devotion, almost worship, it naturally lifts its chin, puts its shoulders back, steps out with a spring, and glances down confidently upon the whole world. Who wouldn't?"[68]

The great American pageant of equality has had many European spectators over the two centuries it has been in progress. They often arrived with their minds already made up—that the famous experiment in egalitarianism was a success or that it was a failure, or that it was destined to succeed or it was doomed to fail. The bulk of the spectators came with a certain amount of skepticism. They generally found what they were looking for. For every boasted success in the pursuit of equality there was a glaring failure, and for every triumph there was a farce, a fraud, a paradox, or an anomaly.

A century ago equality could still be seen by a few not merely as an American goal, hope, or ideal but as a reality already achieved. Thus in 1883 one optimist declared that, "The equality which exists in American society is infinitely more real than persons living in Europe can understand," a reality largely the result of social leveling achieved by the public schools.[69] More common was the view that reality was being drained out of the egalitarian faith by "the growth of a very rich class at one end of the line, and a very poor class at the other end."[70] André Siegfried concluded in 1927 that "the

[68] Arnold Bennett, *Your United States* (New York and London, 1912), 147–48, 153.
[69] Adams, *Our American Cousins*, 331.
[70] Bryce, *American Commonwealth*, II, 601.

Americans have lost all sincere convictions concerning the equality of all men," as manifest by their racial biases.[71] For Aldous Huxley the grotesque efforts to maintain the hypothesis "that all men are equal and that I am just as good as you are" had become a preposterous pretense. "It is so manifestly untrue that a most elaborate system of humbug has been invented in order to render it credible to any normal sane human being. Nowhere has this system of humbug been brought to such perfection as in America."[72] G. K. Chesterton thought that "equality is still the ideal though no longer the reality of America." The struggle to make it reality still continued, however, and "upon the issue of that struggle depends the question of whether this great new civilization continues to exist, and even whether any one cares if it exists or not."[73]

Tocqueville had warned that "men will never establish any equality with which they can be contented," that "the desire for equality always becomes more insatiable in proportion as equality is more complete," that attainment "perpetually retires from before them yet without hiding itself from their sight, and in retiring draws them on. At every moment they think they are about to grasp it; it escapes at every moment from their hold."[74] It would seem that this eternally repetitious drama of Tantalus Americanus and his endless and painful strivings for equality would have eventually palled and lost the attention of its foreign audience. Instead the audience has grown and attention would seem assured so long as Tantalus continues his efforts.

[71] André Siegfried, *America Comes of Age* (New York, 1927), 35.
[72] Huxley, *Jesting Pilate*, 276.
[73] Chesterton, *What I Saw*, 45.
[74] Tocqueville, *Democracy in America*, II, 138–39.

Acknowledgments

The ideas, thoughts, and impressions from which this book eventually grew were accumulated and sorted out over a period of time. Some were inspired by the friends of European birth and education and colleagues of like origins one is privileged to acquire during a long academic career. Those who found refuge in American universities before, during, and after the Second World War were an exceptionally stimulating generation. Other sources derive from brief residence, academic assignments, or visits and tours in Europe. In the main, however, as the annotation of the book indicates, my reliance has always been upon reading what Europeans, either long before my time or beyond my ken and acquaintance, have written about America. It was not reading of the sort or the amount that could best be done in one concentrated spell. But over a period of years, while other work went forward, the notes accumulated, and one book joined another as my shelves became crowded with volumes quite different from those on my regular historical interests.

The opportunity and necessity of putting these thoughts together in writing came in the form of an attractive invitation to inaugurate in 1990 an annual American Lectures Series jointly sponsored by the New York Public Library and the Oxford University Press, to be delivered at the Library and published by the Press and the Library. While no part of this book has previously appeared in print, some parts originated in

132 ACKNOWLEDGMENTS

lectures given on other occasions. The first was one of an hour's length for the Jefferson Lecture Series sponsored by the National Endowment for the Humanities and delivered at the Library of Congress in 1978. The last one, appearing here under the title "Russo-American Counterpoint," was inspired by an invitation to give a lecture in 1990 at universities in Leningrad and Moscow. None of these is duplicated here, but some of their themes are used. In the New York Public Library-Oxford Press lectures I attempted to present in brief form the ideas and evidence I had by then accumulated on the subject. These lectures have been expanded by illustrations, examples, and annotated evidence to form this book. For her invaluable editing, this book, as have several previous ones, owes much to Leona Capeless, my longtime editor at the Oxford University Press.

My indebtedness to the published work of others is, I hope, adequately acknowledged in notes to the text. For debts of a more personal kind there is no adequate way to give acknowledgment. I would at least like to thank Peter Gay for his generous help in reading, listening, and advising, and George Wilson Pierson, the great Tocqueville scholar, for the flow of his learning and wisdom over many years of colleague-ship. An early version of four of the chapters profited greatly from a critical reading by the late Robert Penn Warren.

New Haven   C.V.W.
June 1991

Index